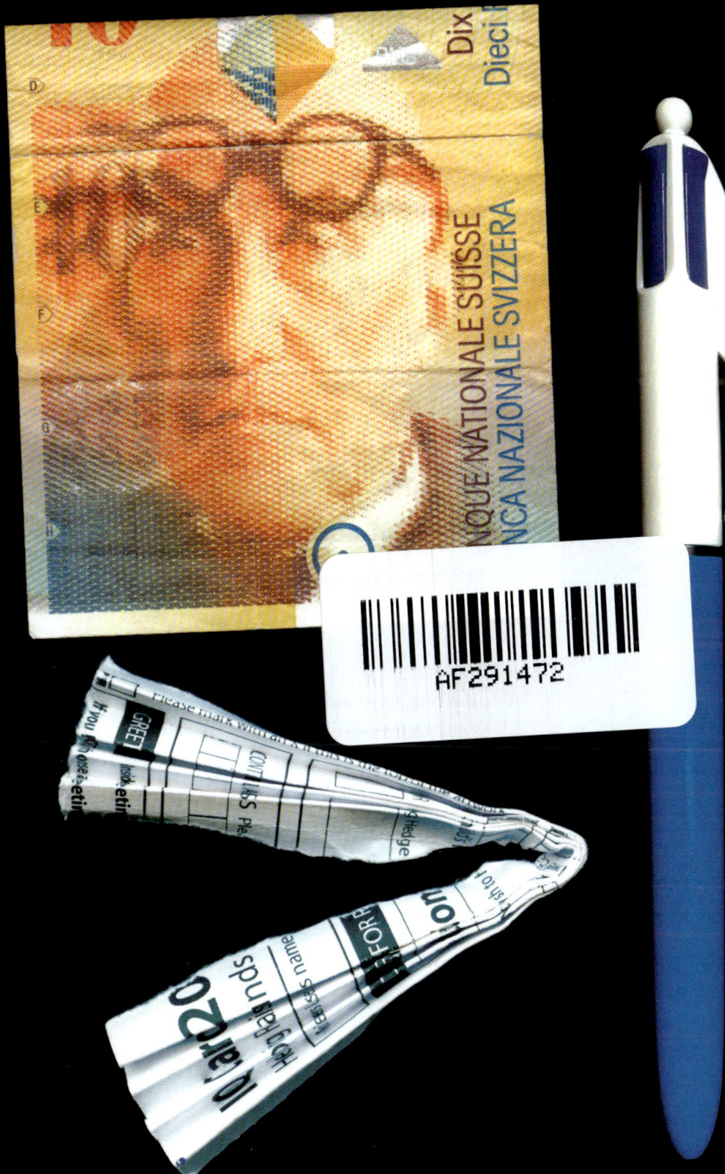

Dix
Dieci
NQUE NATIONALE SUISSE
NCA NAZIONALE SVIZZERA
AF291472
GREET
CONTI ASS
FOR
Please mark with an X if this is the top line of which
If you go through one meeting
ntains name
10 fr 20

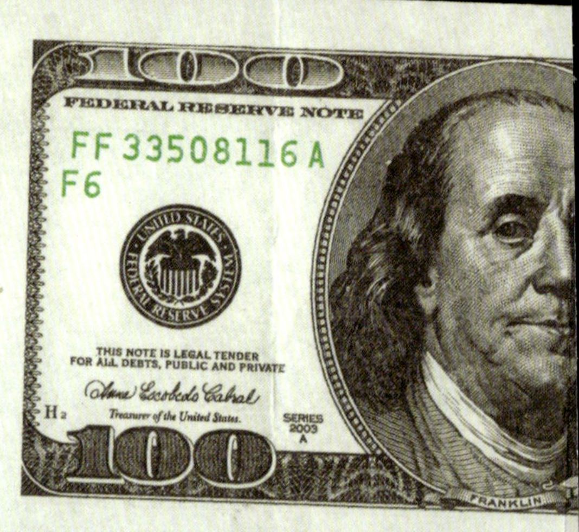

CONFEDERATE GOLD COINS

On April 29, 1861, Superintendent Elmore forwarded a design to Secretary Memminger. This design was prepared by the New Orleans architectural firm of Messers. Gallier & Esterbrook. The description which accompanied this design is as follows:

"...The principal figure, the Goddess of Liberty... in her right hand a... the liberty cap; ...rests on a shield (there being no coat of arms yet adopted) is shown a portion of

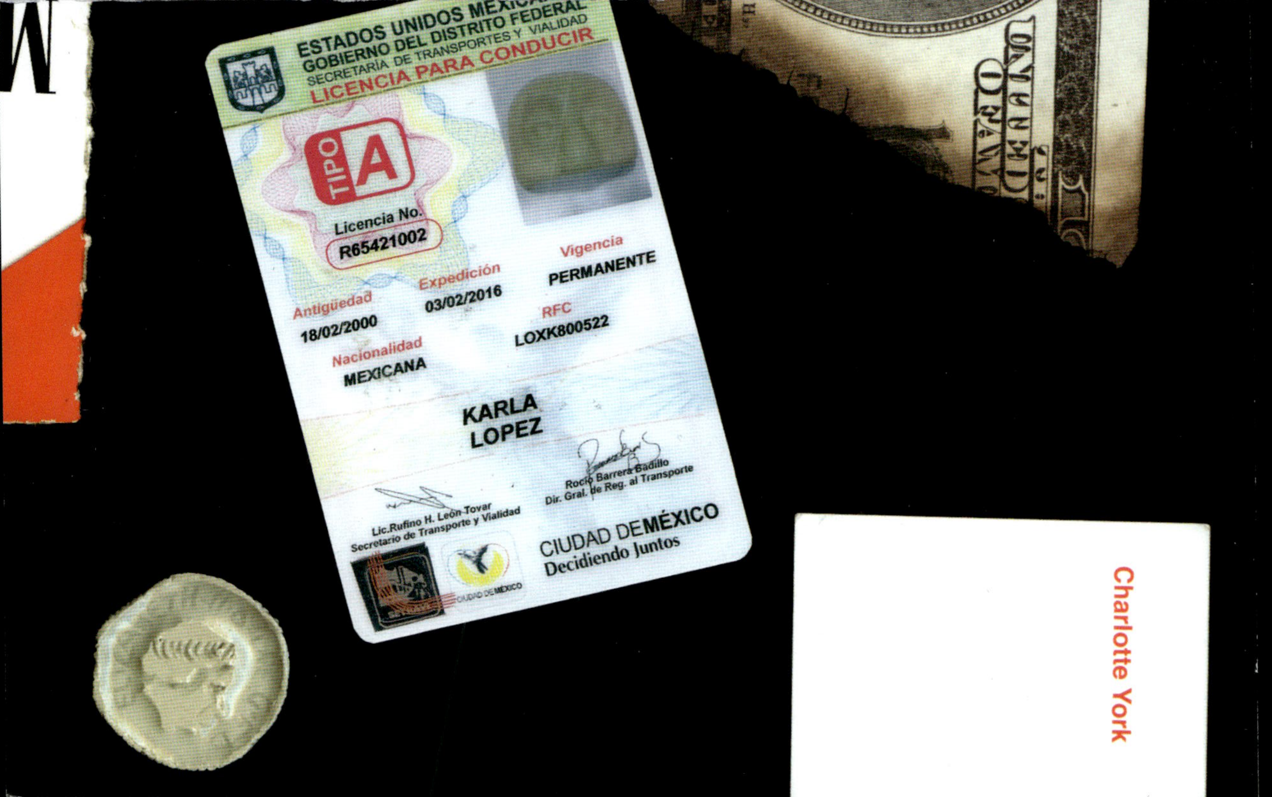

ESTADOS UNIDOS MEXICANOS
GOBIERNO DEL DISTRITO FEDERAL
SECRETARÍA DE TRANSPORTES Y VIALIDAD
LICENCIA PARA CONDUCIR
TIPO A
Licencia No.
R65421002
Antigüedad
18/02/2000
Expedición
03/02/2016
Vigencia
PERMANENTE
RFC
LOXK800522
Nacionalidad
MEXICANA
KARLA
LOPEZ
Lic. Rufino H. León Tovar
Secretario de Transporte y Vialidad
Rocío Barrera Badillo
Dir. Gral. de Reg. al Transporte
CIUDAD DE MÉXICO
Decidiendo Juntos
CIUDAD DE MEXICO
Charlotte York

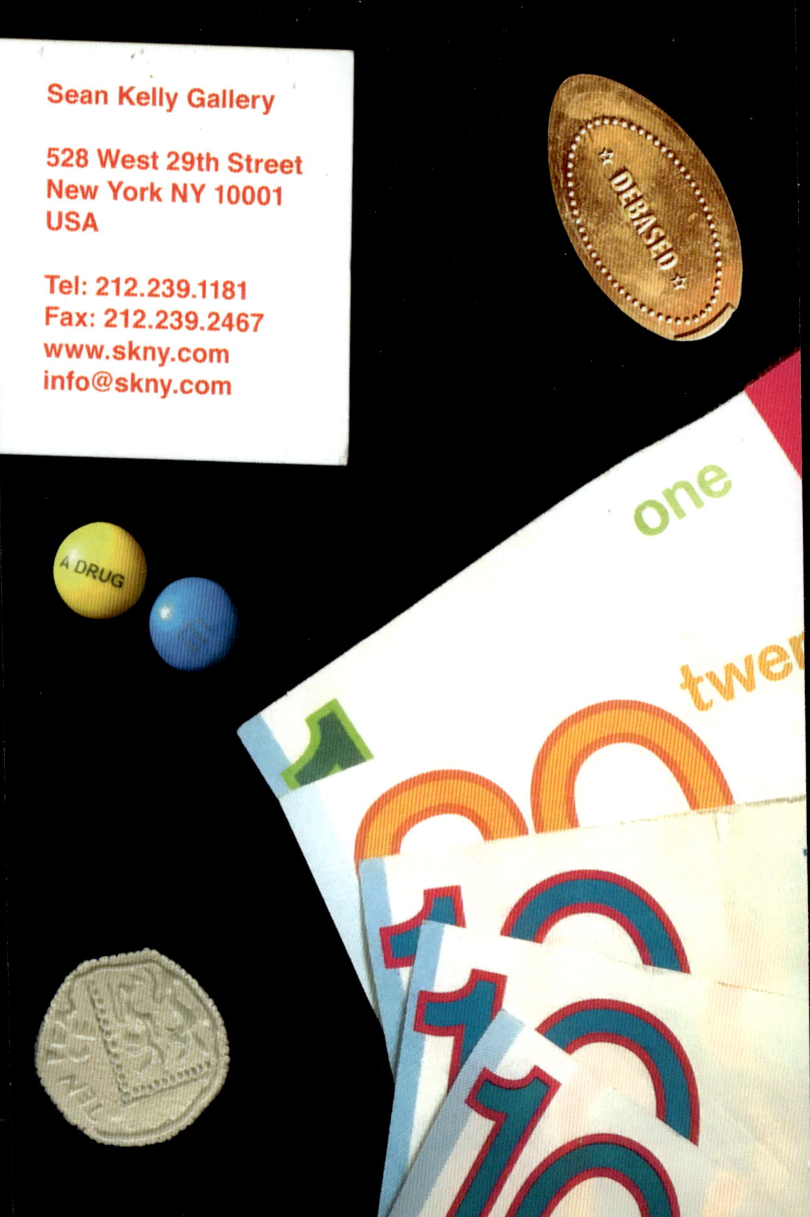
Sean Kelly Gallery

528 West 29th Street
New York NY 10001
USA

Tel: 212.239.1181
Fax: 212.239.2467
www.skny.com
info@skny.com

DEBASED

A DRUG

one

twen

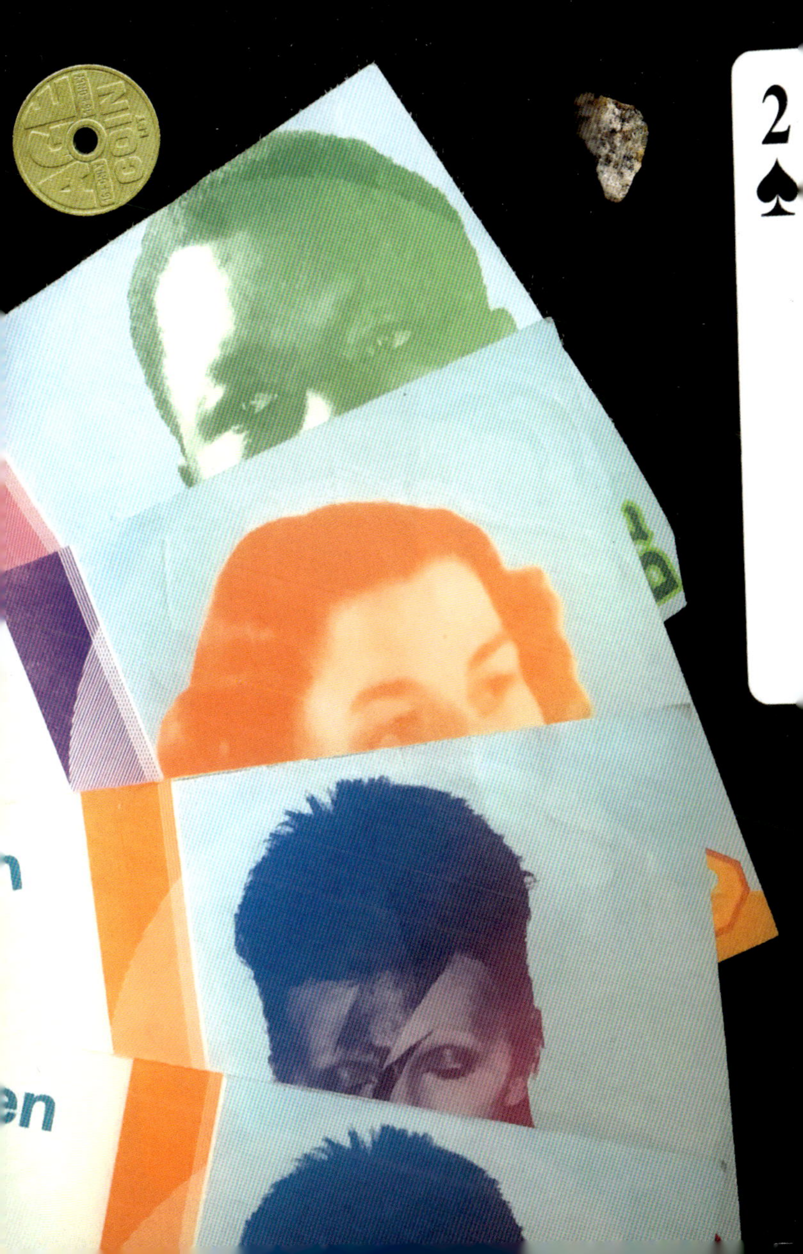

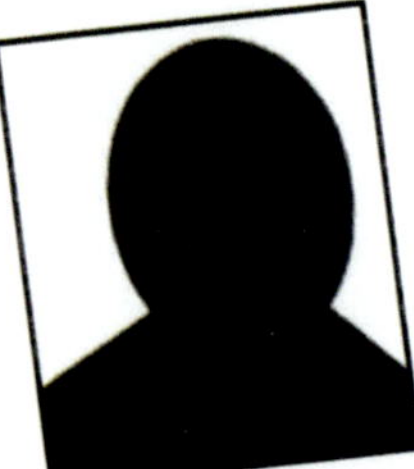

RASHID TAAN KAZIM
Ba'th Party Regional
Chairman for Al-Anbar
Governorate

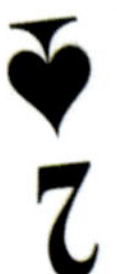

Yaïr Barelli

100, avenue Ledru R
75011 Paris

+33(0)6.64.91.65.50

Donorcard ("the Artwork")
Carey Young ("the Artist")
2005
Ink on paper
Unique (from a series of 3000
produced for Arte Contempo,
Frieze Art Fair, 2009)

In consideration of the donation of this card
to me by the Artist, I hereby agree that this
object will only become an artwork by her
upon the inclusion of my signature, and that
it will retain its status as an artwork solely
for the duration of the Artist's life, or my
life, whichever is the shorter.

Signature ________________________ Date ________

Full name ________________________________
(BLOCK CAPITALS)

Artist's signature _____ Date 18/10/2009

In the event of my death please contact:

Name ________________ Tel. ________
(BLOCK CAPITALS)   (INTERNATIONAL DIALLING CODE)

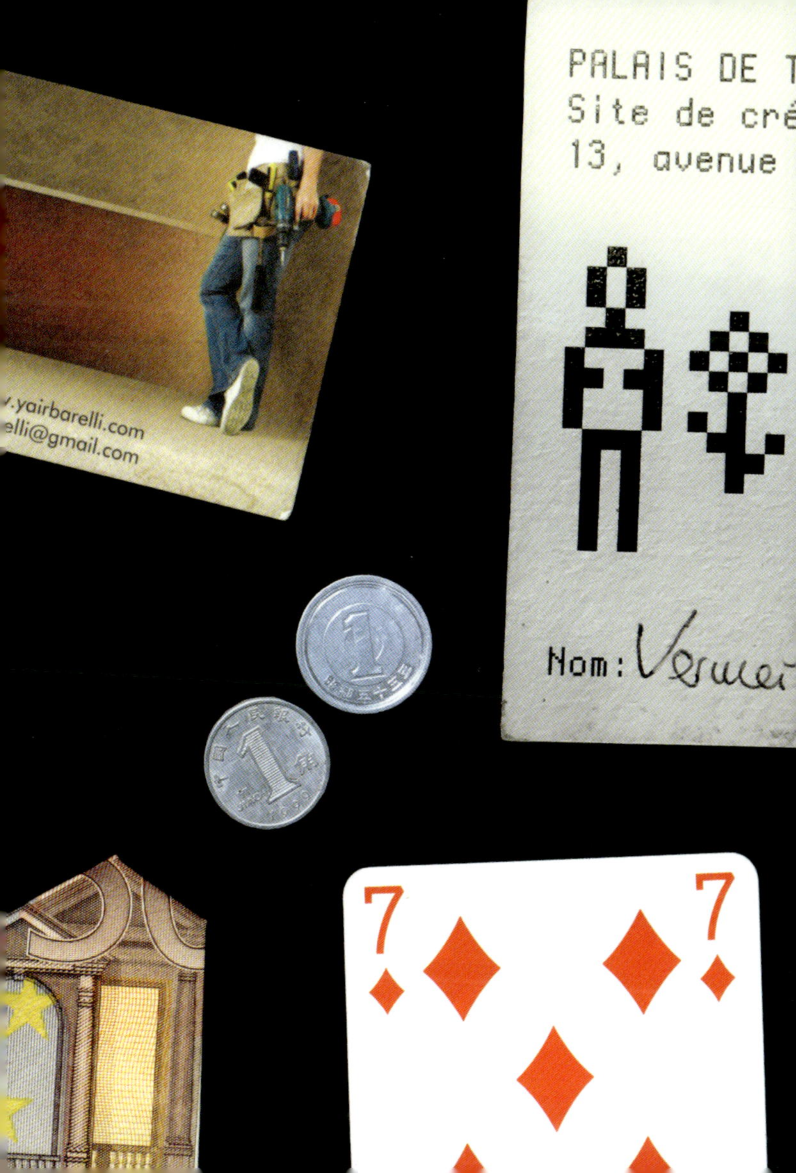
v.yairbarelli.com
elli@gmail.com
PALAIS DE T
Site de cré
13, avenue
Nom: Vermei
7 7

OKYO,
ation contemporaine
du Président Wilson F-75116 Paris

LAISSEZ-PASSER PERMANENT
POUR DEUX PERSONNES

Prénom: Samuel

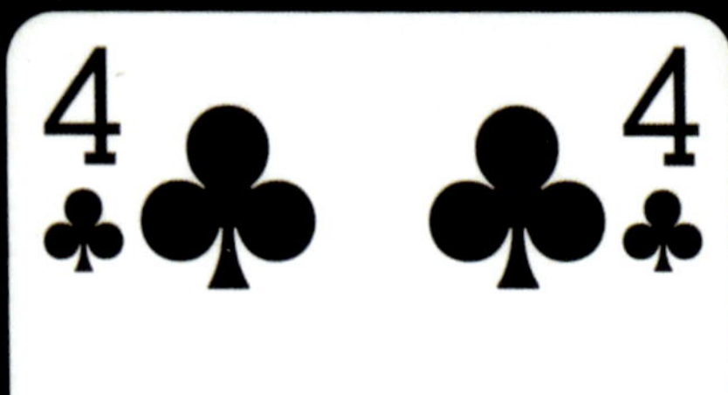

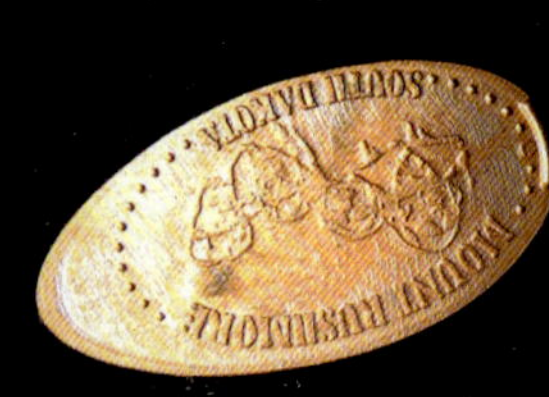

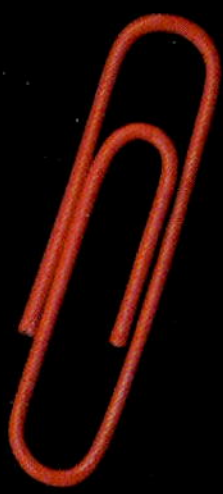

Arthur Lloyd

Human Card Index

Any printed items on request

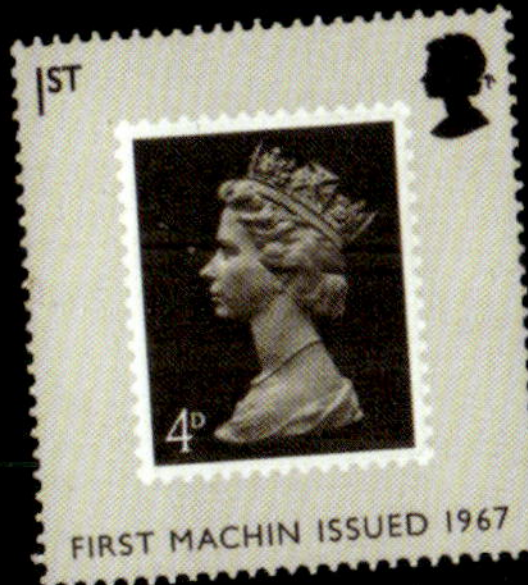

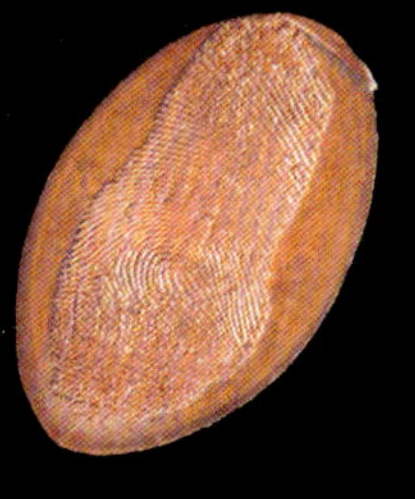

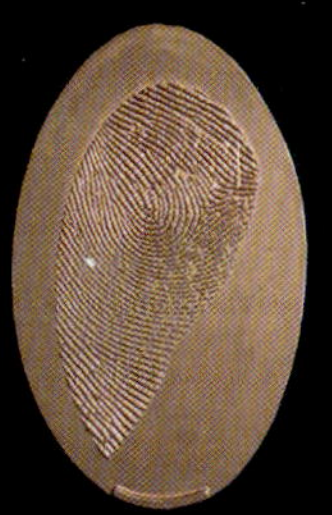

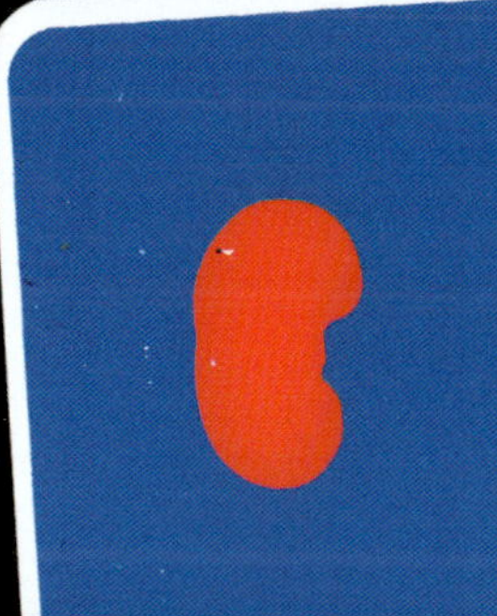

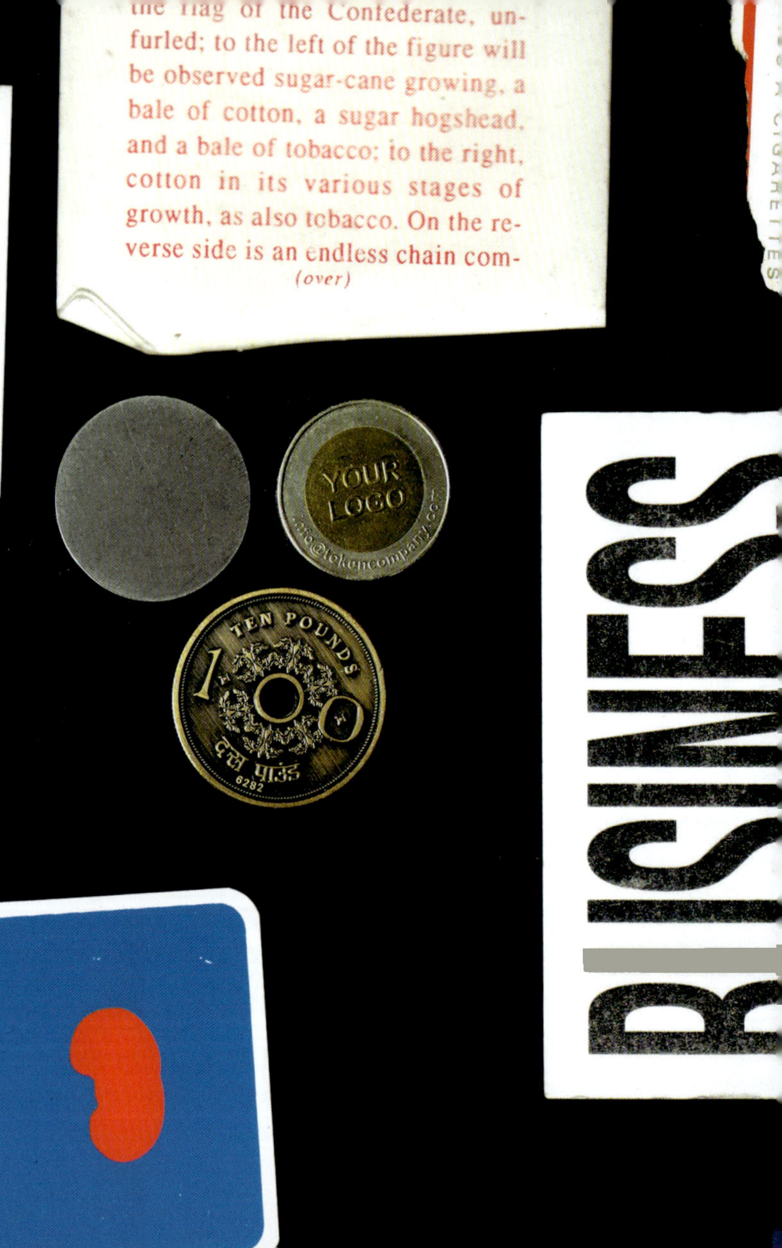
the flag of the Confederate, un-
furled; to the left of the figure will
be observed sugar-cane growing, a
bale of cotton, a sugar hogshead,
and a bale of tobacco: to the right,
cotton in its various stages of
growth, as also tobacco. On the reverse side is an endless chain com-
(over)
YOUR LOGO
info@tokencompany.com
TEN POUNDS
1 00
6282
BUSINESS

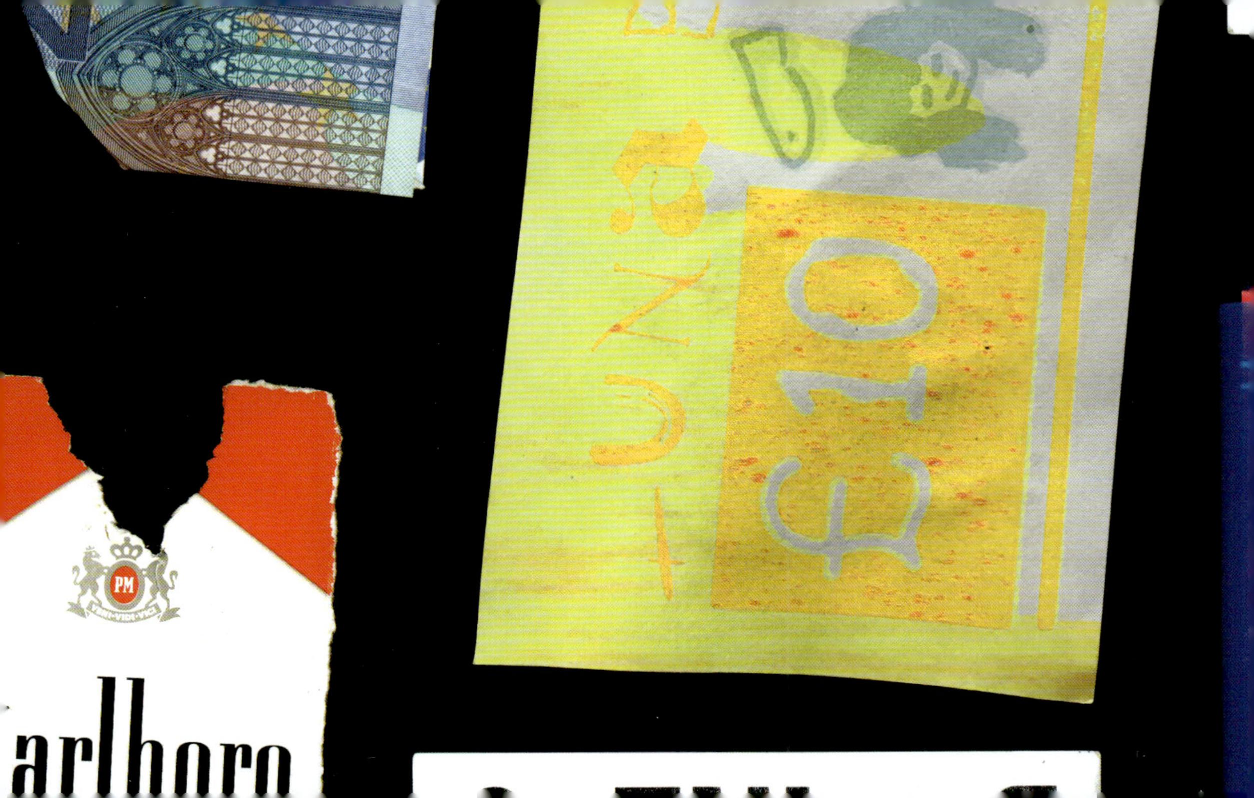

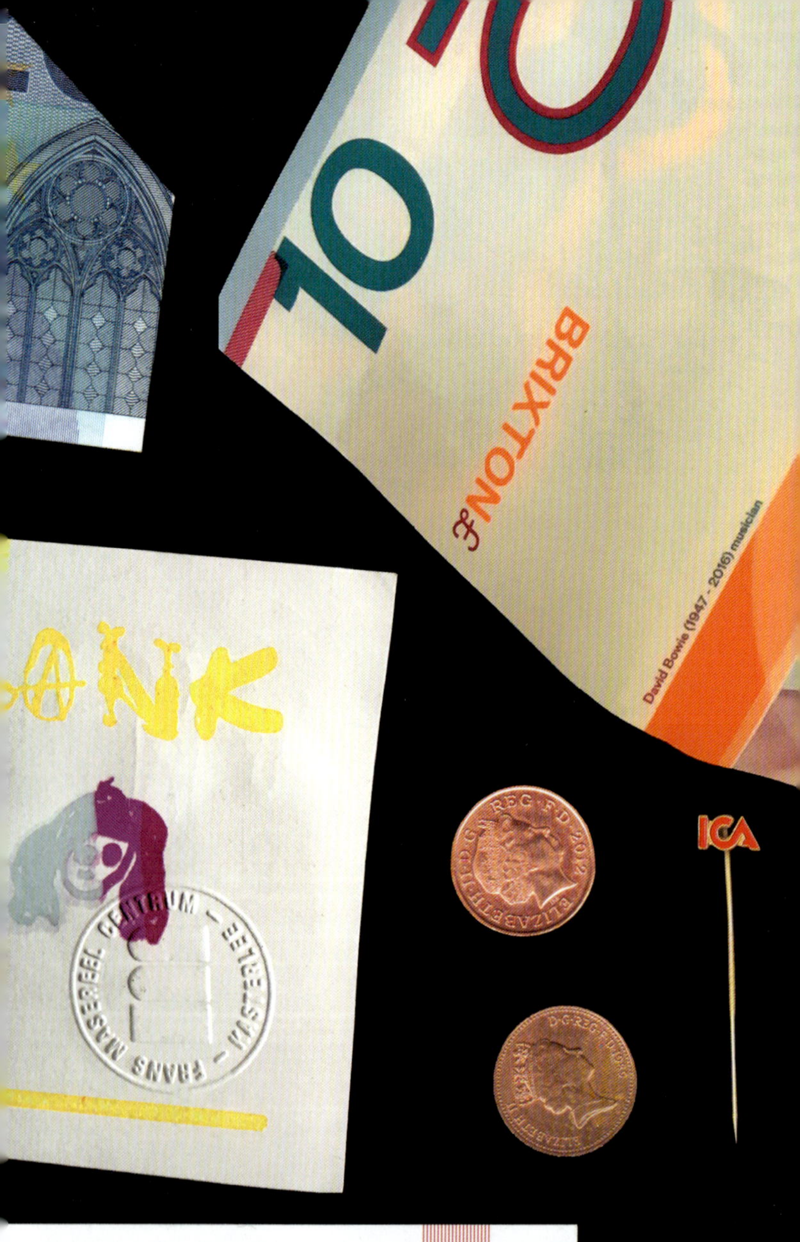

BRIXTON
David Bowie (1947 - 2016) musician
ANK
FRANS MASEREEL CENTRUM - KASTERLEE
ELIZABETH II D.G.REG.F.D. 2012
D.G.REG.F.D. 2013
ELIZABETH II
ICA

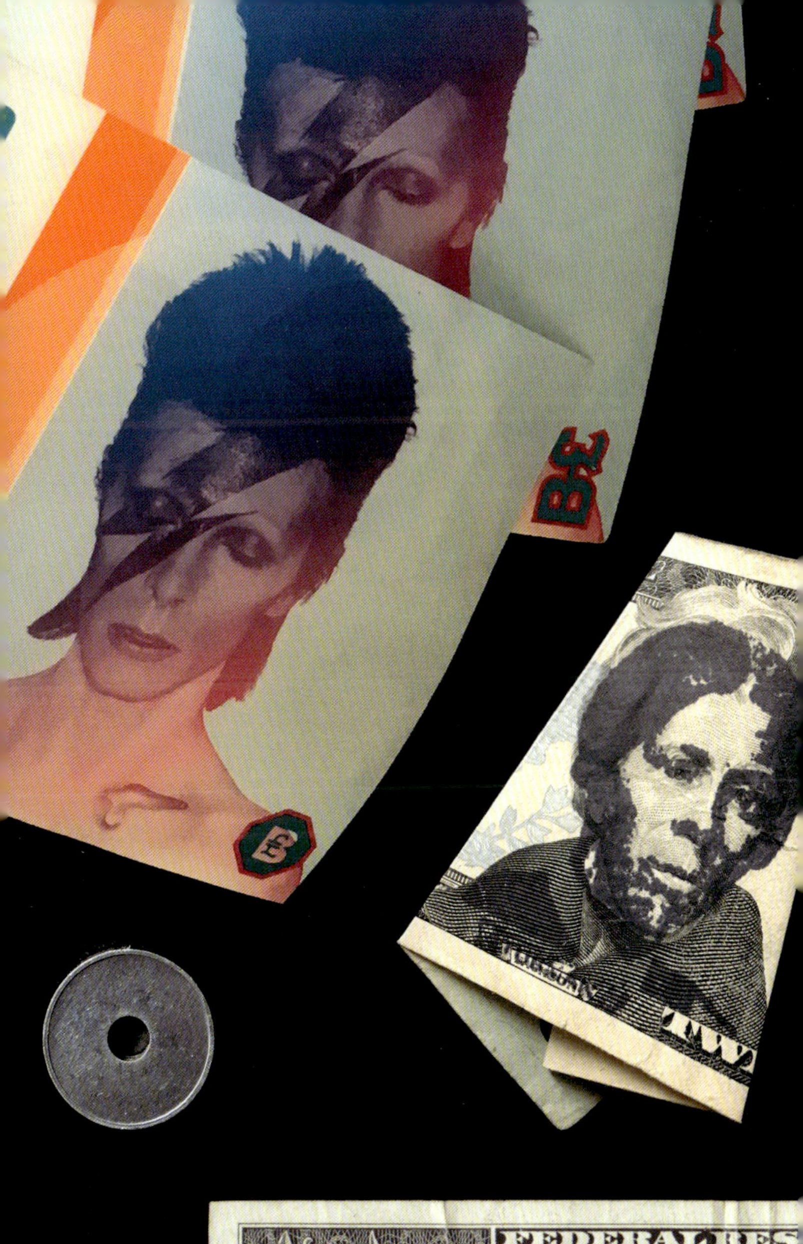
FEDERAL RES

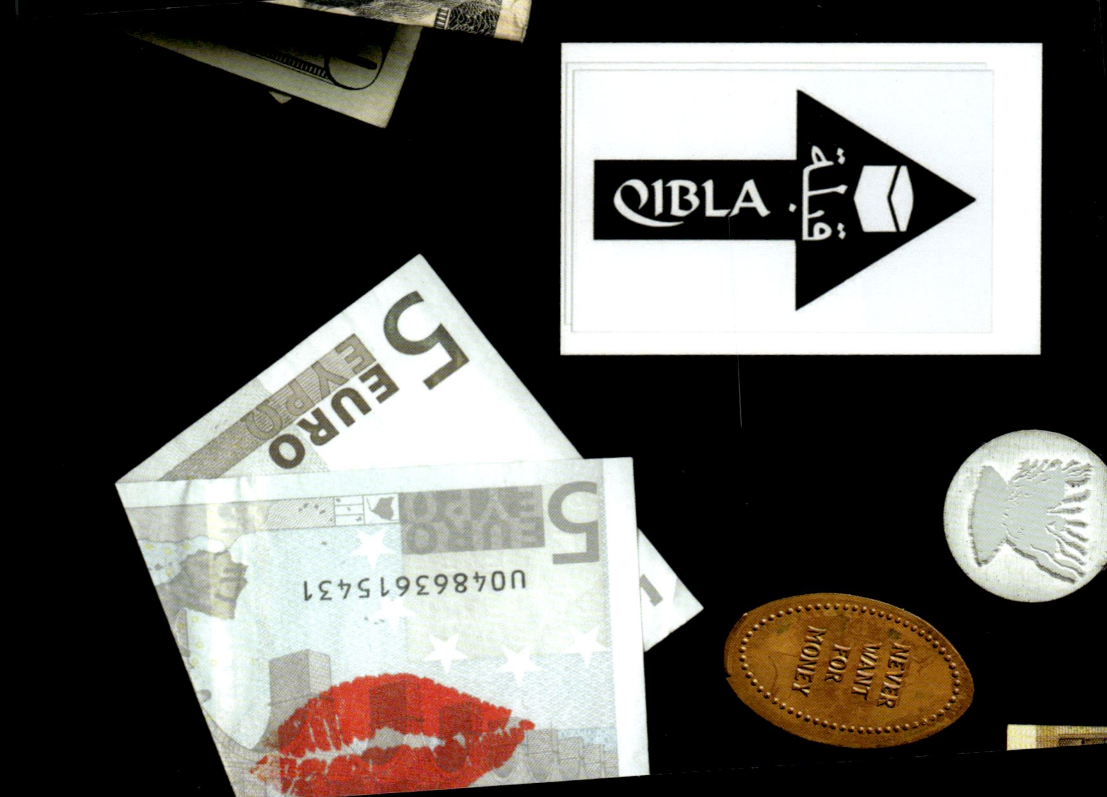
QIBLA ۰ قبلة
5 EURO
5 EURO
U04863615431
ERVE NOTE
NEVER WANT FOR MONEY

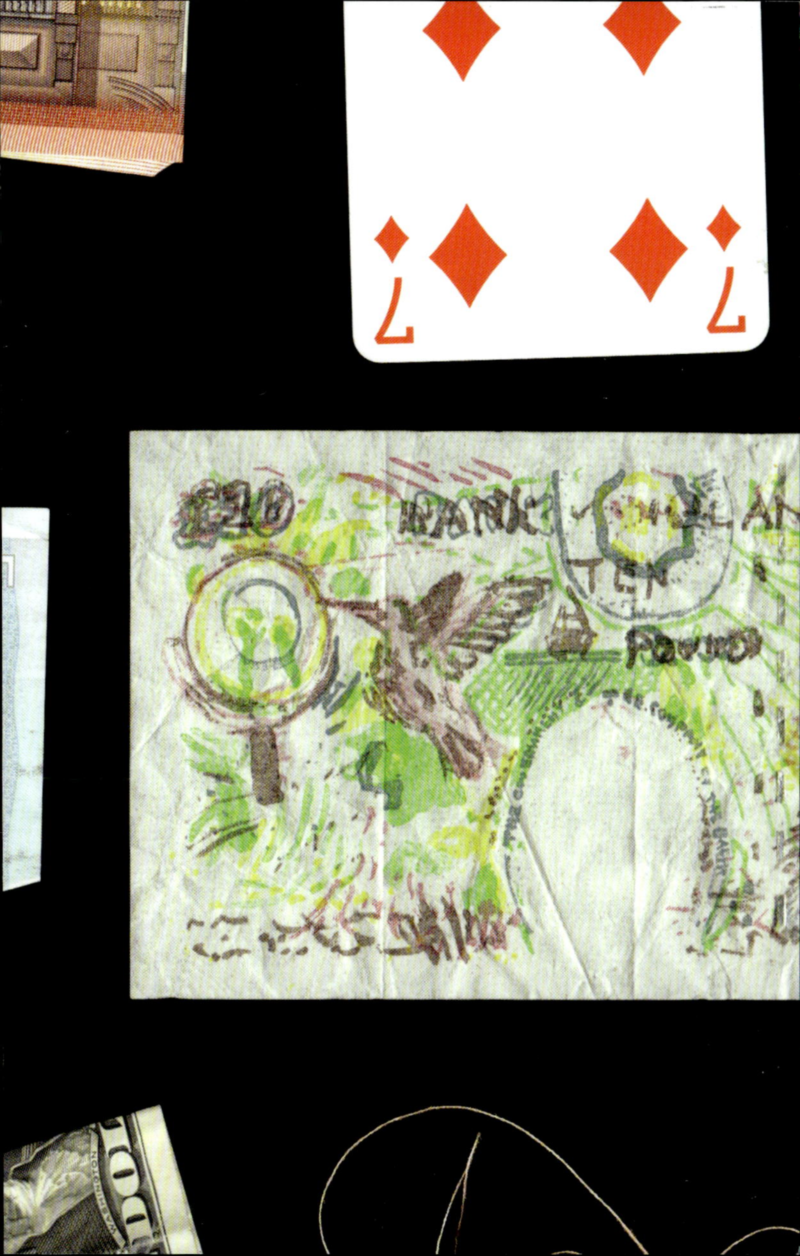

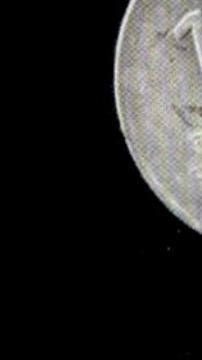
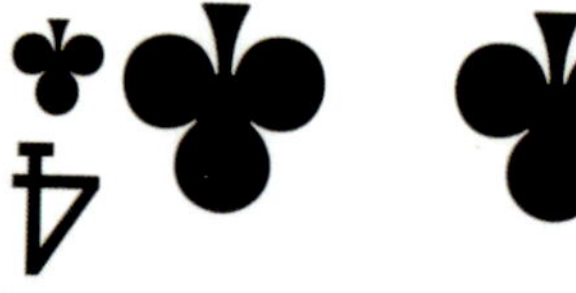
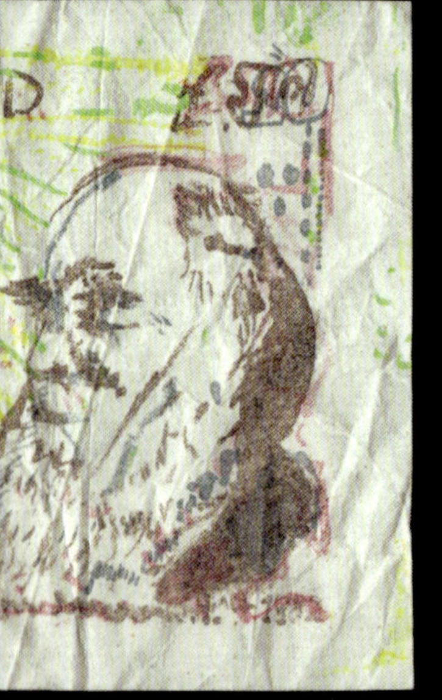
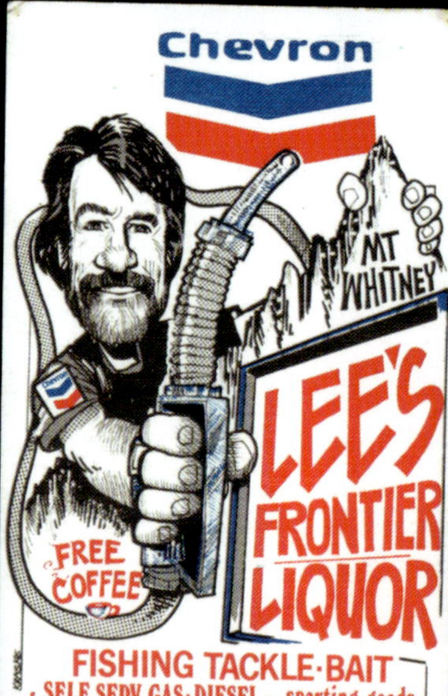

Chevron
MT WHITNEY
FREE COFFEE
LEE'S FRONTIER LIQUOR
FISHING TACKLE·BAIT
· SELF SERV. GAS· DIESEL · sporting goods ·
·LIQUOR·WINE·BEER·DELI· ICE · GUNS·AMMO·
1900 S. Main, Lone Pine, Ca. USA ~ 93545
760 876·5844

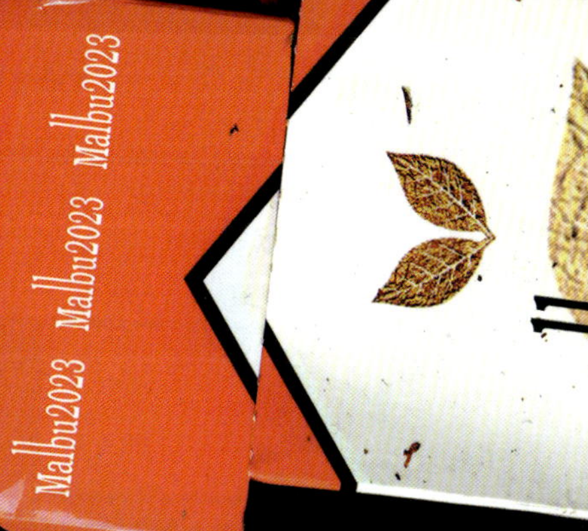
SELECTED PREMIUM TOBACCOS
Malbu2023
Malbu2023
Malbu2023
Malbu2023
Malbu2023
Malbu2023

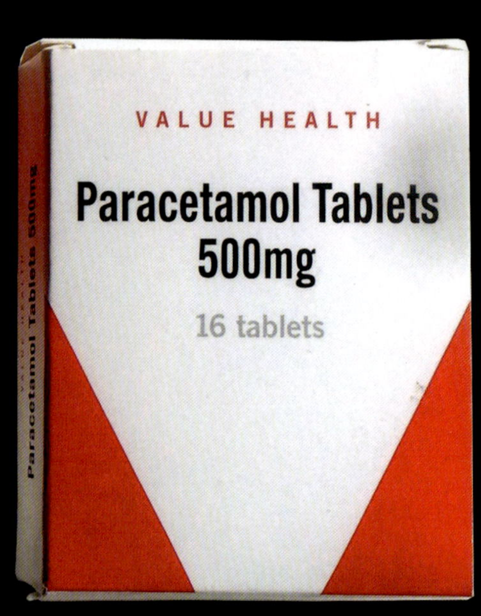
VALUE HEALTH
Paracetamol Tablets 500mg
16 tablets
Paracetamol Tablets 500mg

DE STIJL
Pieter Cornelis Mondriaan
Cypress Hill Cemetary
833 Jamaica Avenue
Brooklyn, NY 11208, USA
+1 718-277-2900

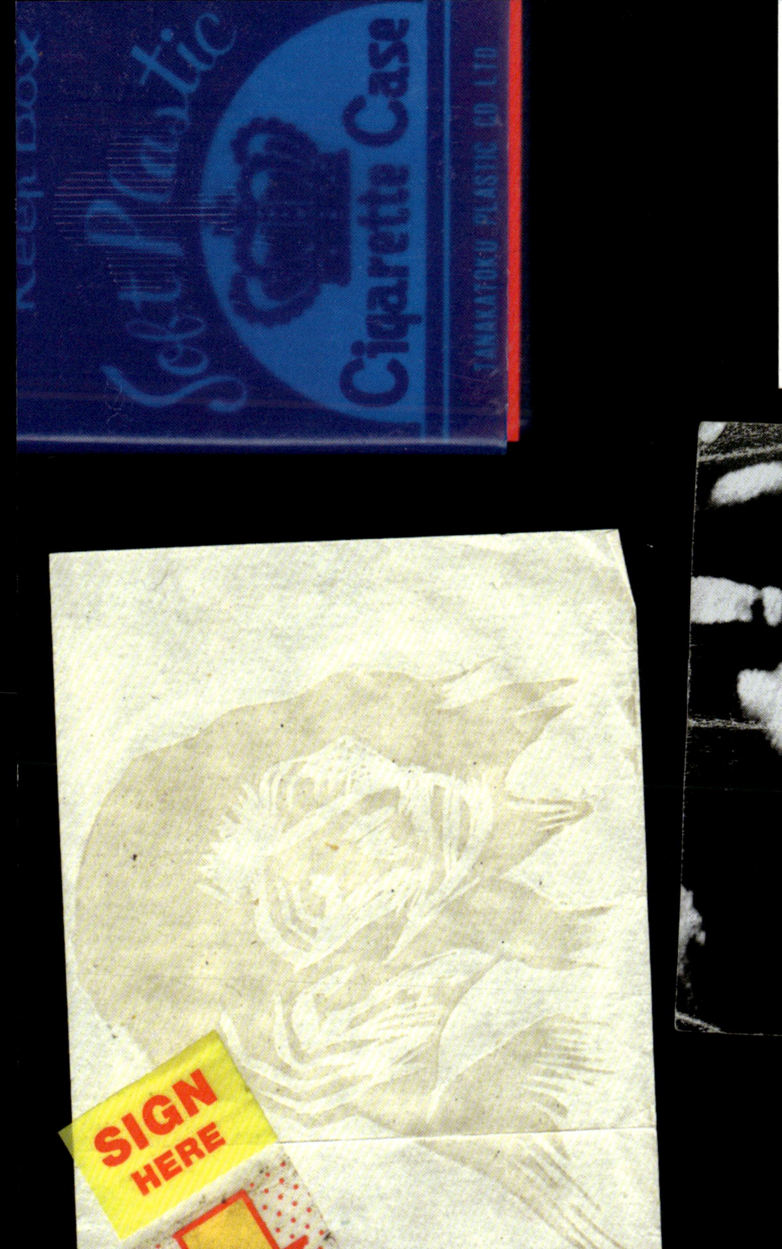
Keep Box
Self Plastic
Cigarette Case
DAIKOKU PLASTIC CO LTD
SIGN
HERE

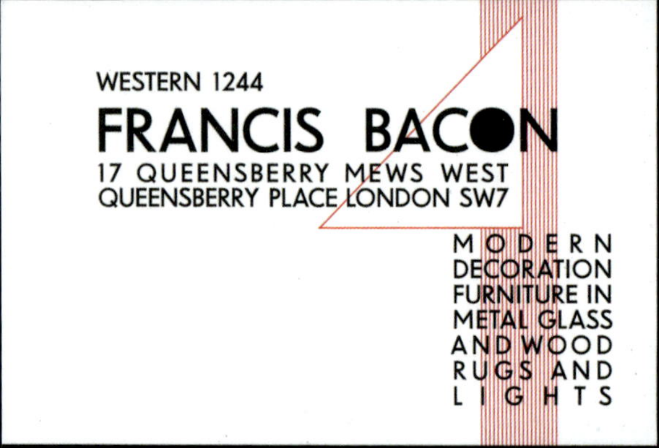

WESTERN 1244

FRANCIS BACON

17 QUEENSBERRY MEWS WEST
QUEENSBERRY PLACE LONDON SW7

MODERN
DECORATION
FURNITURE IN
METAL GLASS
AND WOOD
RUGS AND
LIGHTS

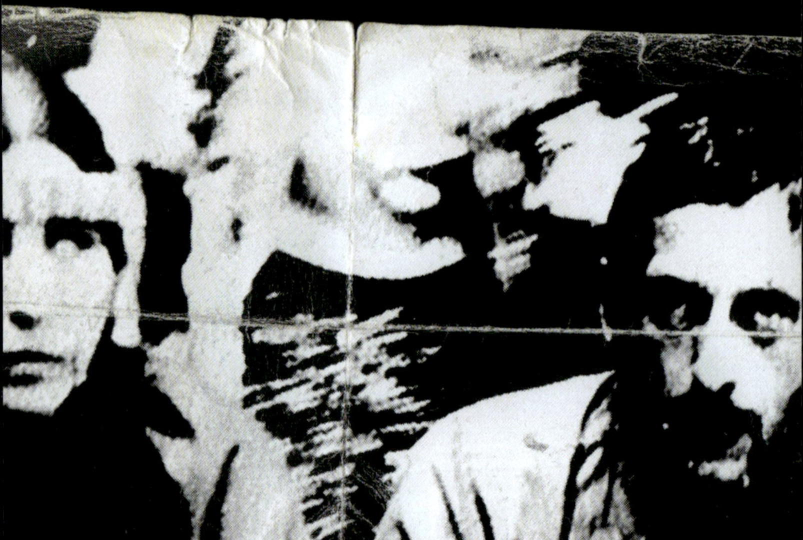

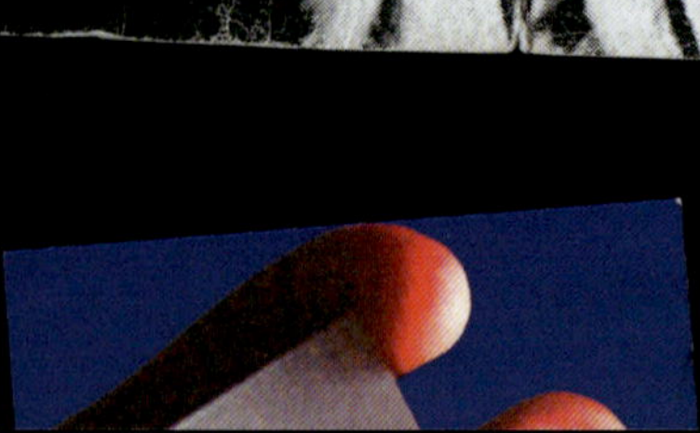

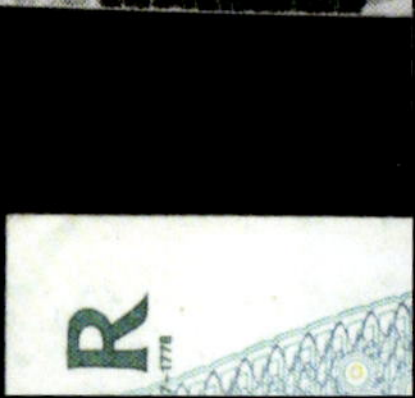

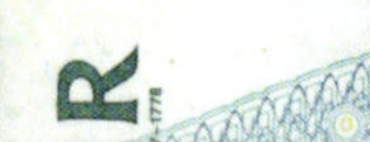

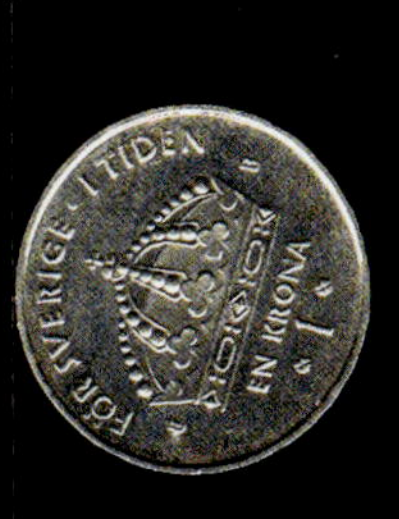

FÖR SVERIGE I TIDEN
EN KRONA
1

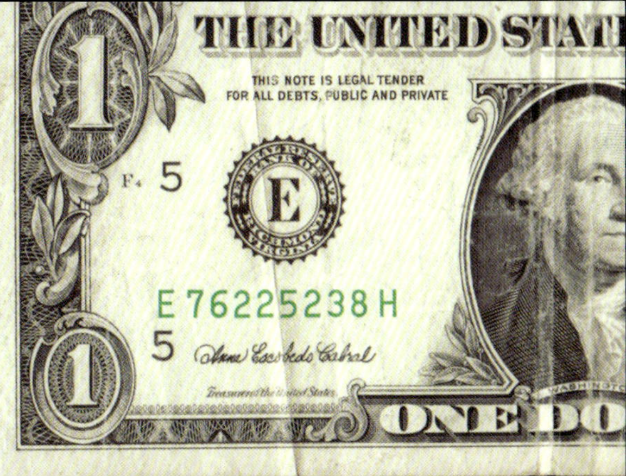

THE UNITED STATE
1
THIS NOTE IS LEGAL TENDER
FOR ALL DEBTS, PUBLIC AND PRIVATE
F4 5
E
E 76225238 H
5
Anna Escobedo Cabral
Treasurer of the United States
ONE DO
1

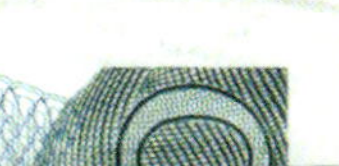

MUSÉE OCÉANOGRAPHIQUE DE MONACO
2017 - 2
0
EURO
SOUV
ENIR
0
NAVIRE
Seconde Princesse-Alice
UE

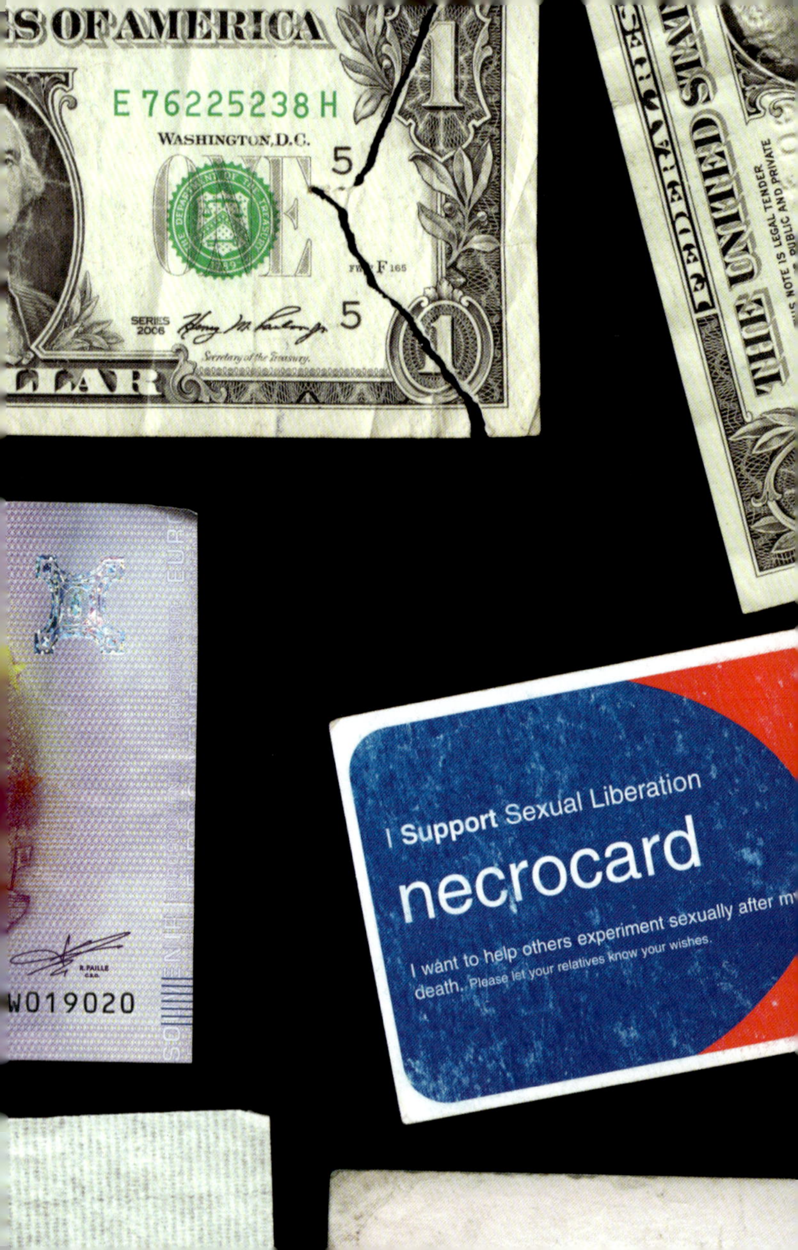
S OF AMERICA
E 76225238 H
WASHINGTON, D.C.
ONE
5
F 165
5
SERIES
2006
Secretary of the Treasury.
LLAR
THE UNITED STA
FEDERAL RES
THIS NOTE IS LEGAL TENDER
PUBLIC AND PRIVATE
EURO
R.PAILLE
W019020
I Support Sexual Liberation
necrocard
I want to help others experiment sexually after my
death. Please let your relatives know your wishes.

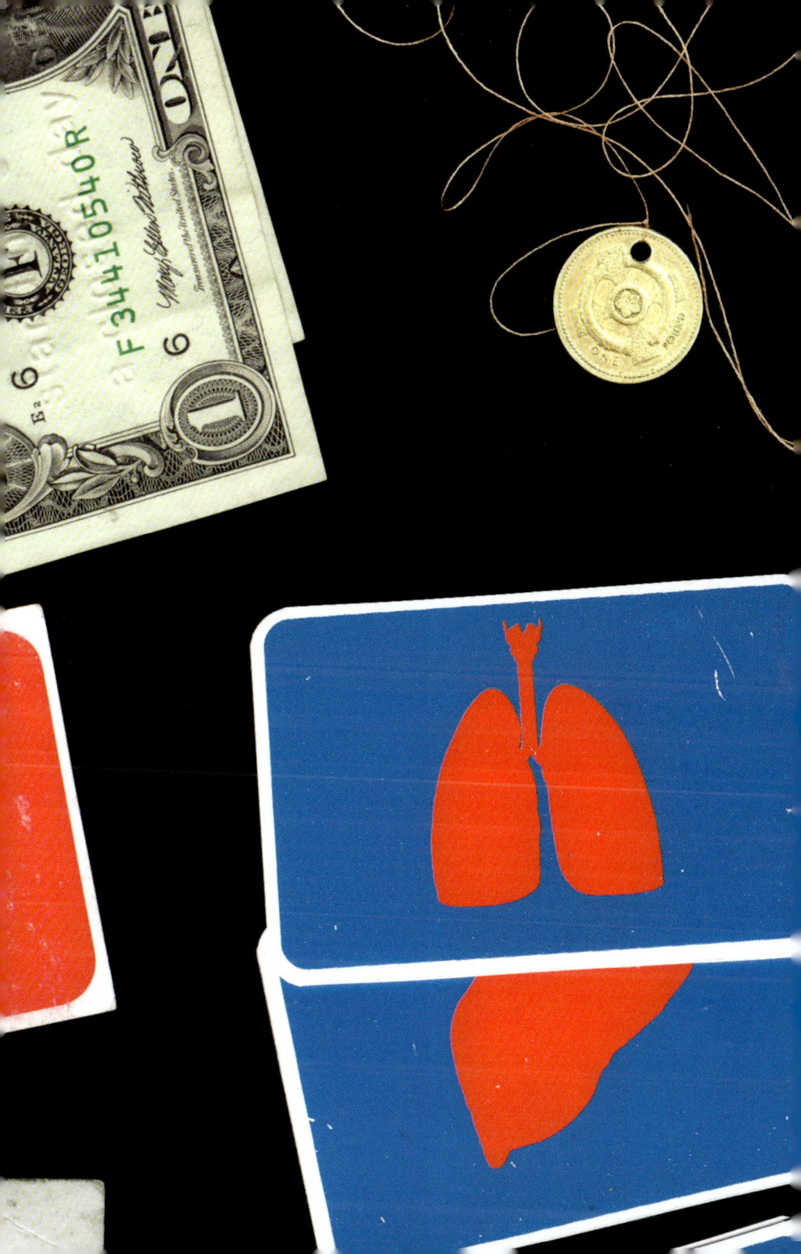

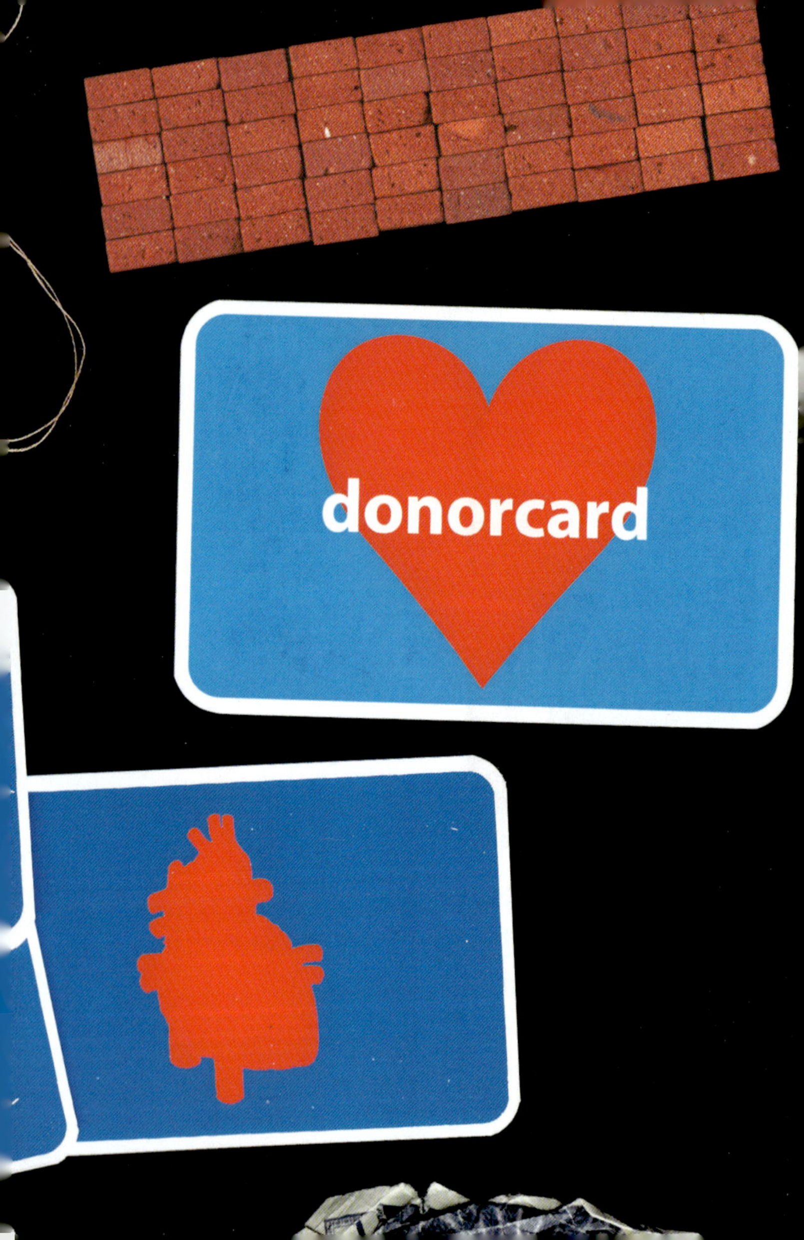
donorcard

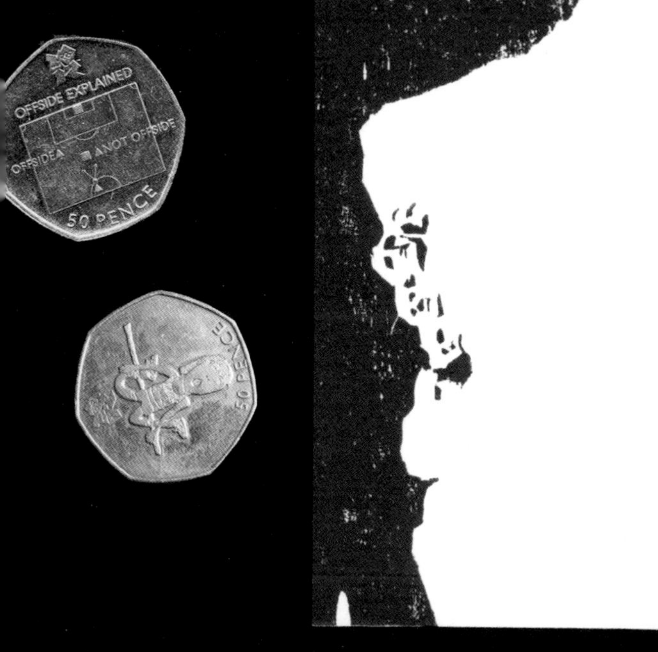

Meet
me
outside

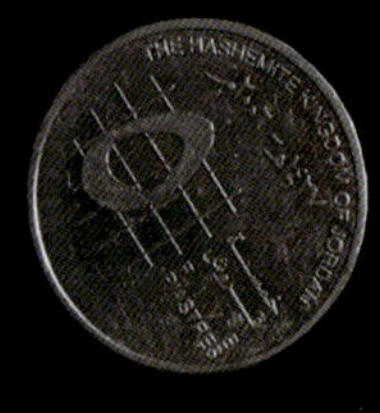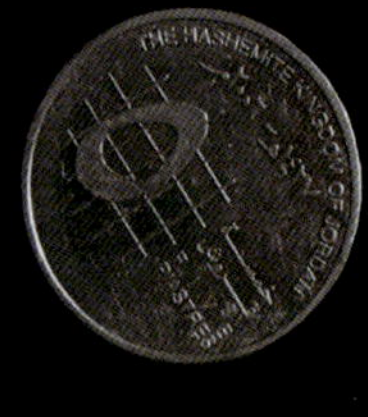

I EAT LUNCH BETWEEN TWO HIGHWAYS

（東京地下鉄）

東京メトロ線

Tsukishima

月 島 ▶ 170 区間

小児 90円

2019.-5.-1

発売当日限り有効

下車前途無効 02

1595 19:59

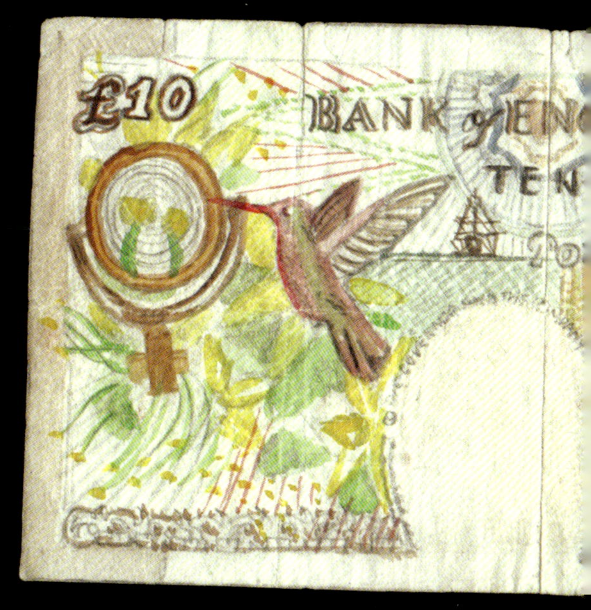
£10
BANK of ENG
TEN

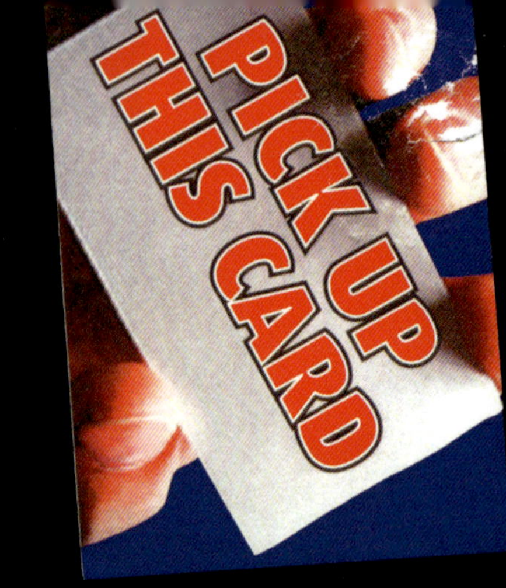
PICK UP
THIS CARD

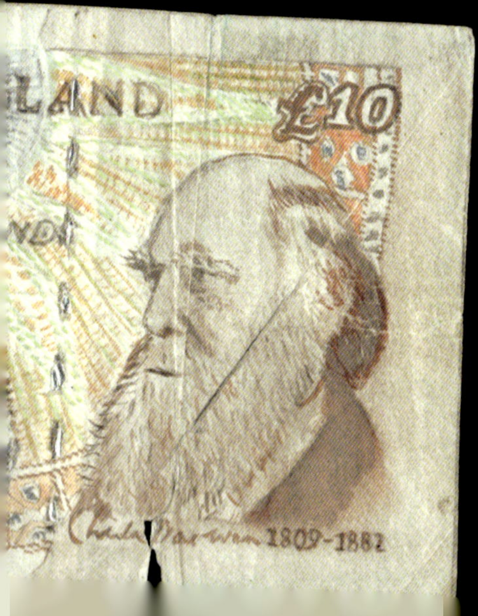
LAND
£10
Charles Darwin 1809-1882

Do you know there was a female emperor in Chinese history? Do you know her name?

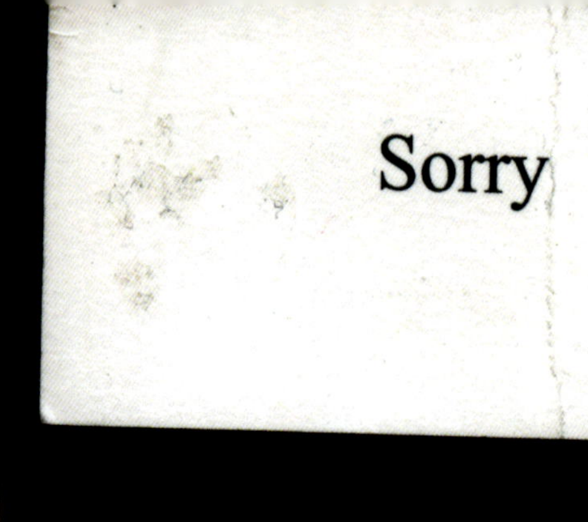
Sorry

HEAD – Genève
Haute école d'art et de design
Bd James-Fazy 15
1201 Geneva, Switzerland
www.hesge.ch/head/

Maki Suzuki
Enseignant / Teacher
Master of Arts
Espace
Space & Communication

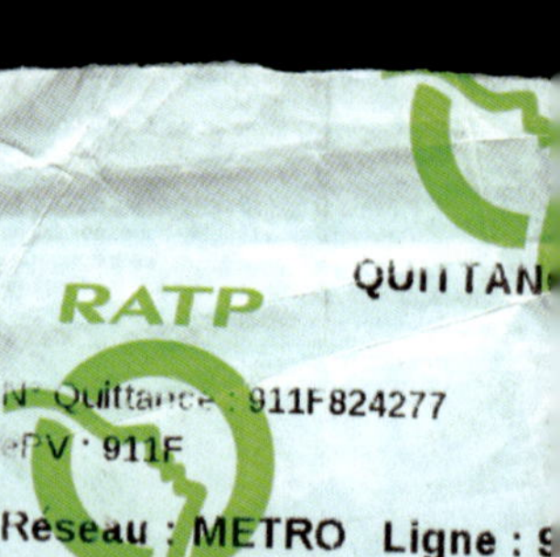
RATP
QUITTAN
N° Quittance : 911F824277
PV : 911F

Réseau : METRO   Ligne : 9
Station : IENA
Commune : PARIS

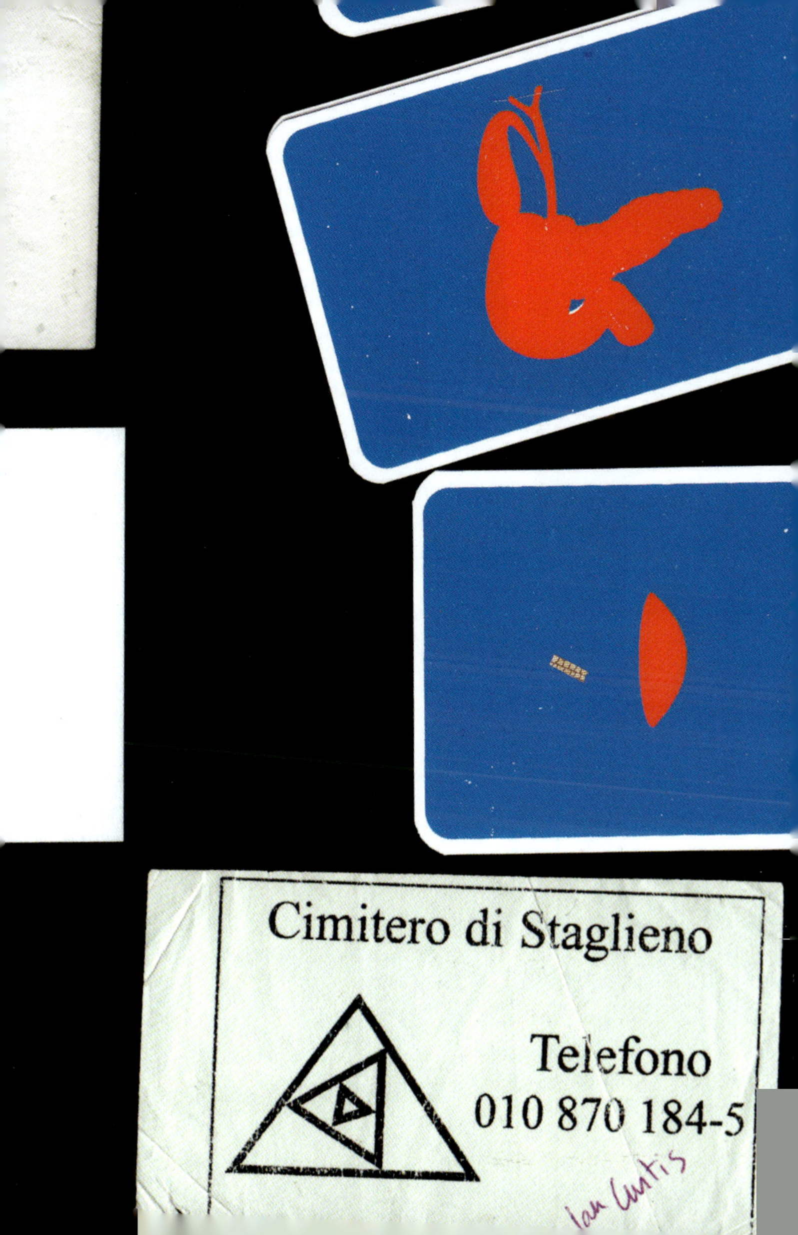

Cimitero di Staglieno
Telefono
010 870 184-5
Ian Curtis

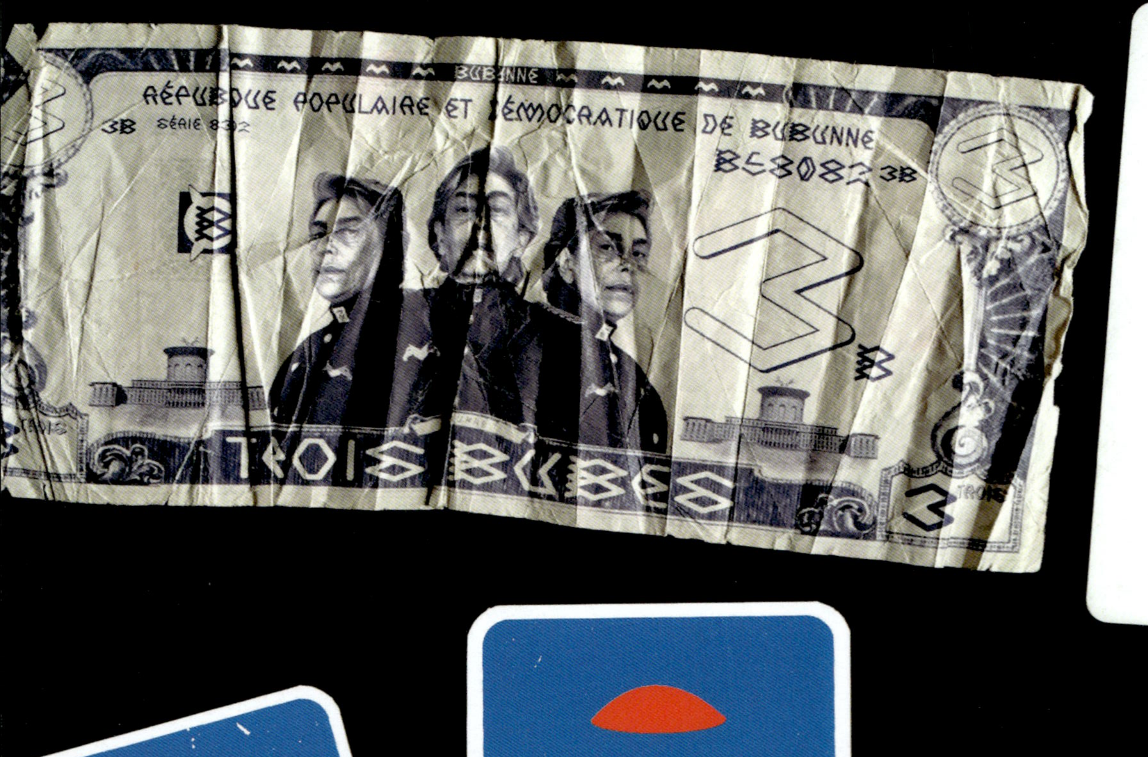
BUBENNE
RÉPUBLIQUE POPULAIRE ET DÉMOCRATIQUE DE BUBENNE
3B SÉRIE 832
BUBENNE 3B
TROIS BUBES
3 TROIS

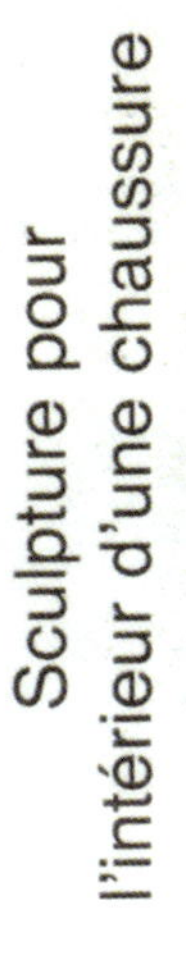

Sculpture pour
l'intérieur d'une chaussure
Uwe Max Jensen 1999

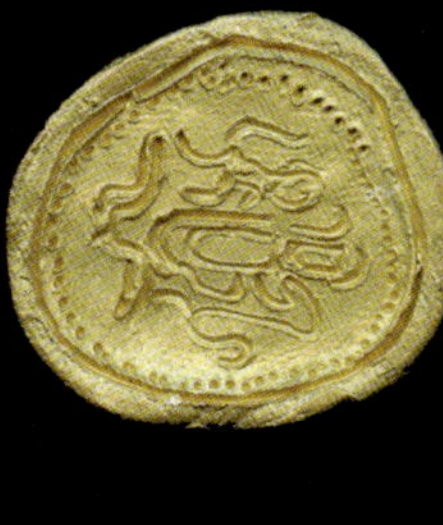

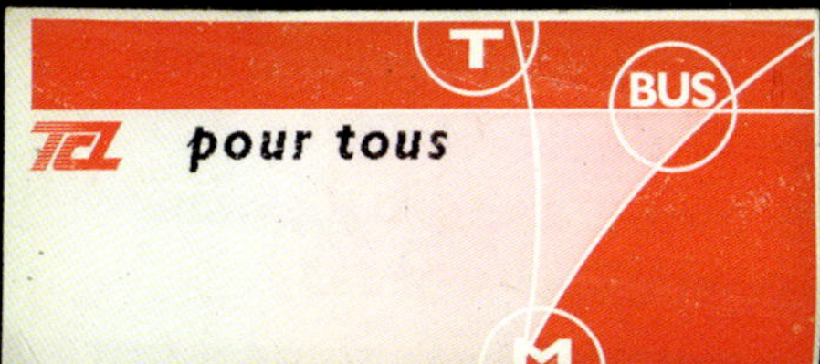

TCL
pour tous
T
BUS
M

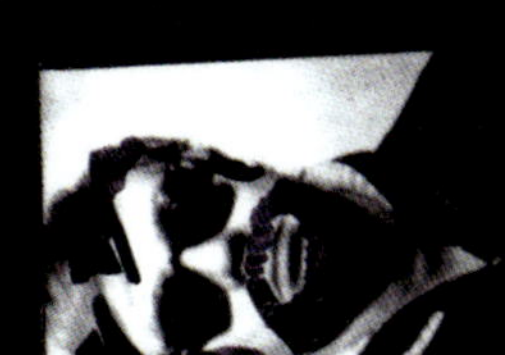

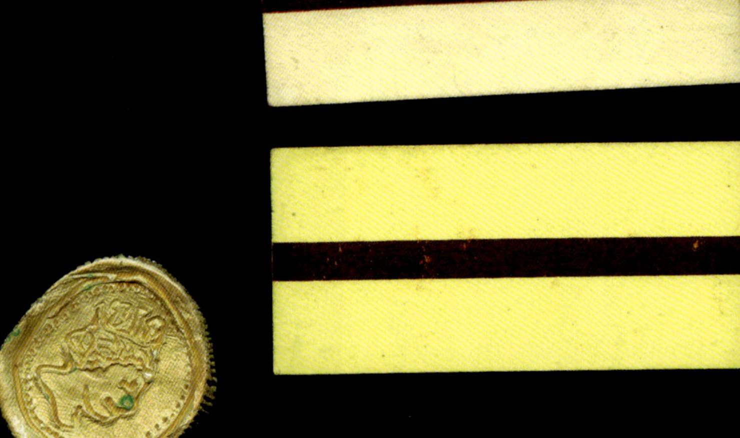

FLIGHT 93 MEMORIAL

As you approach Somerset, follow signs for Rte. 281 North. Take Rte. 281 North for 1.7 miles to US 219 North. Travel 8.7 miles North on US 219 to the Stoystown, Jennerstown, US 30 exit, turn right onto US 30 East. Travel 8.5 miles on US 30 East. Turn right into the new park entrance, which will be marked with official National Park Service signs.

For GPS, use 6424 Lincoln Highway, Stoystown, PA 15563

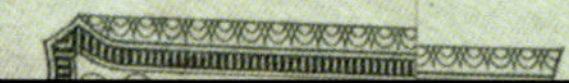

Frans Masereel Centrum
collectief Åbäke als curat
kunst. Met 'All the Knives
in een nagenoeg lege ruim
De inhoud van deze tento
ruimte betreedt en wordt
wereld vol grafiek en graf

FRANS MASEREEL CENTRUM

Z33
Huis voor actuele kunst

**Z33 - huis voor actuele kunst
Zuivelmarkt 33, Hasselt (BE)
www.z33.be**

Z33 is een initiatief van de Provincie Limburg

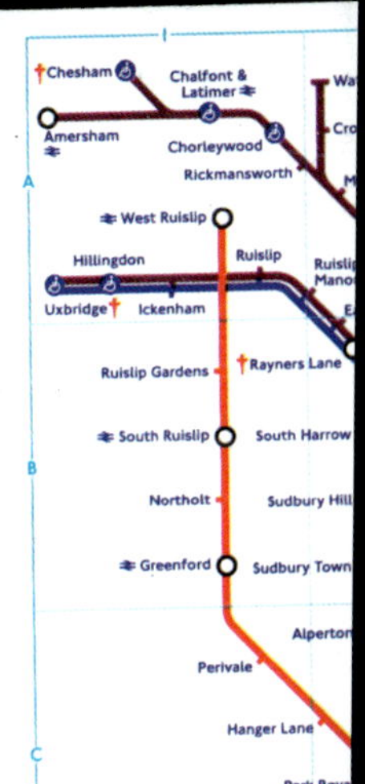

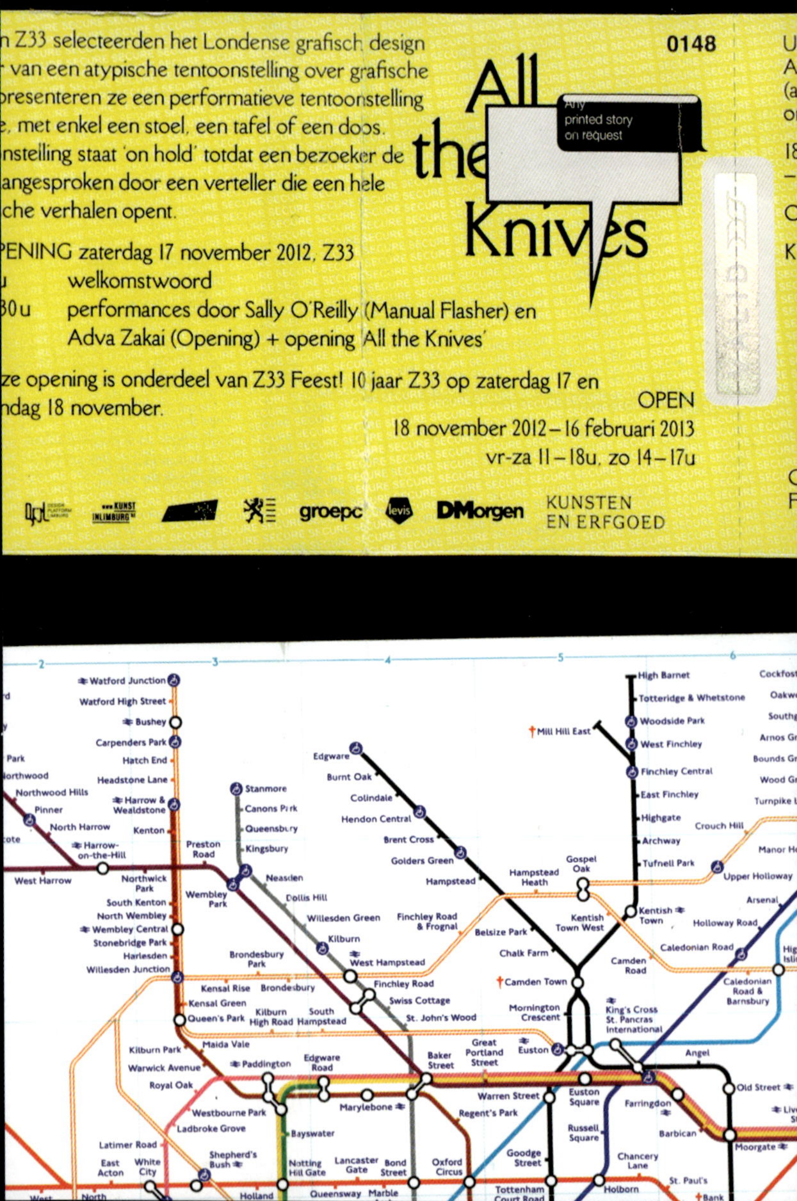
n Z33 selecteerden het Londense grafisch design
r van een atypische tentoonstelling over grafische
resenteren ze een performatieve tentoonstelling
e, met enkel een stoel, een tafel of een doos.
nstelling staat 'on hold' totdat een bezoeker de
angesproken door een verteller die een hele
che verhalen opent.

PENING zaterdag 17 november 2012, Z33
u   welkomstwoord
30 u   performances door Sally O'Reilly (Manual Flasher) en
           Adva Zakai (Opening) + opening 'All the Knives'

ze opening is onderdeel van Z33 Feest! 10 jaar Z33 op zaterdag 17 en
ndag 18 november.

0148

All
the
Knives
Any
printed story
on request

OPEN
18 november 2012 – 16 februari 2013
vr-za 11 – 18u, zo 14 – 17u

groepc   levis   DMorgen   KUNSTEN EN ERFGOED
KUNST IN LIMBURG
DESIGN PLATFORM LIMBURG

GING   0148
KNIVES
d story
2
013
R: Åbäke

NAARS:
Yaïr Barelli
Jochen Dehn
Dirk Elst
élien Froment
limir Ivaneanu
Sally O'Reilly
Matt Rogers
Adva Zakai

UCTIE: Z33
ereel Centrum

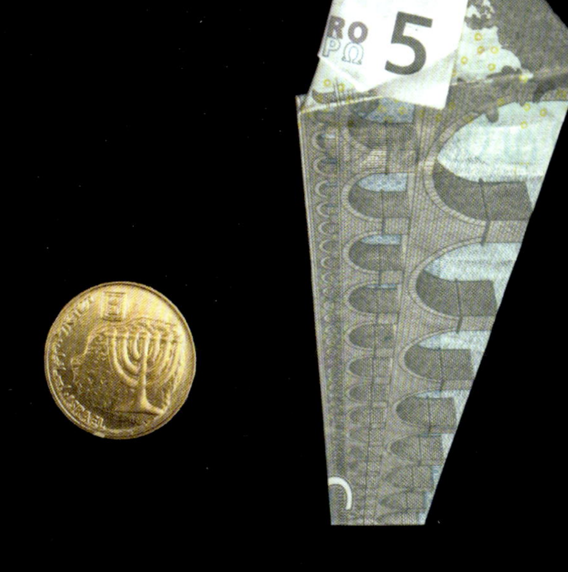
RO 5
EURO

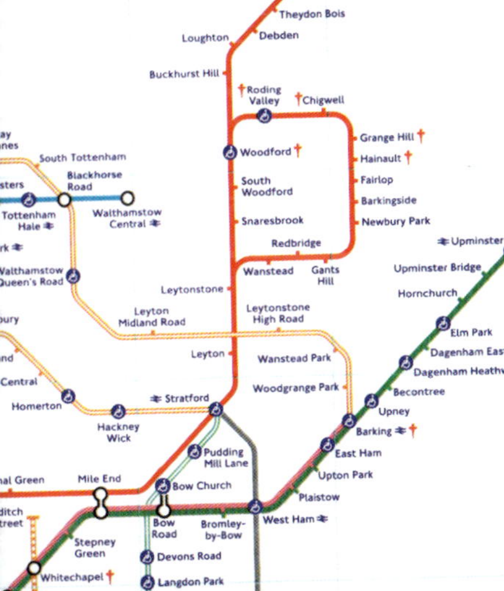
7
8
9
A
B
C
Epping
Theydon Bois
Loughton
Debden
Buckhurst Hill
Roding Valley
Chigwell
Grange Hill
Woodford
Hainault
South Woodford
Fairlop
Barkingside
Snaresbrook
Newbury Park
Redbridge
Upminster
Wanstead
Gants Hill
Upminster Bridge
Leytonstone
Hornchurch
Leyton Midland Road
Leytonstone High Road
Elm Park
Leyton
Wanstead Park
Dagenham East
Dagenham Heathway
Woodgrange Park
Becontree
Central
Upney
Homerton
Stratford
Barking
Hackney Wick
East Ham
Pudding Mill Lane
Upton Park
al Green
Mile End
Bow Church
Plaistow
West Ham
ditch treet
Bow Road
Bromley-by-Bow
Stepney Green
Devons Road
Whitechapel
Langdon Park
South Tottenham
Blackhorse Road
ay nes
sters
Tottenham Hale
Walthamstow Central
rk
Walthamstow Queen's Road
bury
nd

[...]   We all lean over and inspect David's card and Price quietly says, "That's *really* nice." A brief spasm of jealousy courses through me when I notice the elegance of the color and the classy type. I clench my fist as Van Patten says, smugly, "Eggshell with Romalian type..." He turns to me. "What do you think?" ¶"Nice," I croak, but manage to nod, as the busboy brings four fresh Bellinis. ¶"Jesus," Price says, holding the card up to the light, ignoring the new drinks. "This is really super. How'd a nitwit like you get so tasteful?" ¶I'm looking at Van Patten's card and then at mine and cannot believe that Price actually like Van Patten's better. Dizzy, I sip my drink then take a deep breath. ¶"But wait," Price says. "You ain't seen nothin' yet..." He pulls his out of an inside coat pocket and slowly, dramatically turns it over for our inspection and says, "Mine." ¶Even I have to admit it's magnificent. ¶Suddenly the restaurant seems far away, hushed, the noise distant, a meaningless hum, compared to this card, and we all hear Price's words: "Raised lettering, pale nimbus white..." ¶"Holy shit," Van Patten exclaims. "I've never seen..." ¶"Nice, very nice," I have to admit. "But wait. Let's see Montgomery's." ¶Price pulls it out and though he's acting nonchalant, I don't see how he can ignore its subtle off-white coloring, its tasteful thickness. I am unexpectedly depressed that I started this.   [...]

Date : 30/08/2018 Heure : 12

Infraction : 6027 titre de transport
non validé art.5-1° et art.15-1° Déc
03.05.2016
Montant de l'infraction : 35,00€
Paiement espèces : 35,00€

Confiscation Titre : NON

Matricule agent : 725122

La quittance constitue un titre de transport et
correspond au versement d'une indemnité
forfaitaire, à titre de transaction libératoire de tou
poursuite, en application des articles 529-3 et 529
du code de procédure pénale et du décret du 22
mars 1942.

RATP

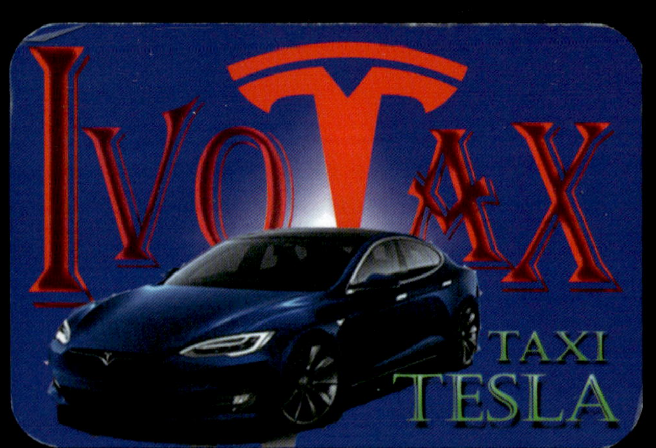

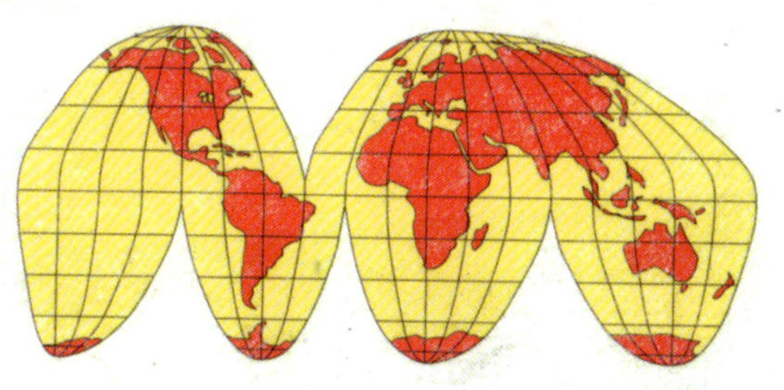
NO FORMULA ONE NO CRY TAXI

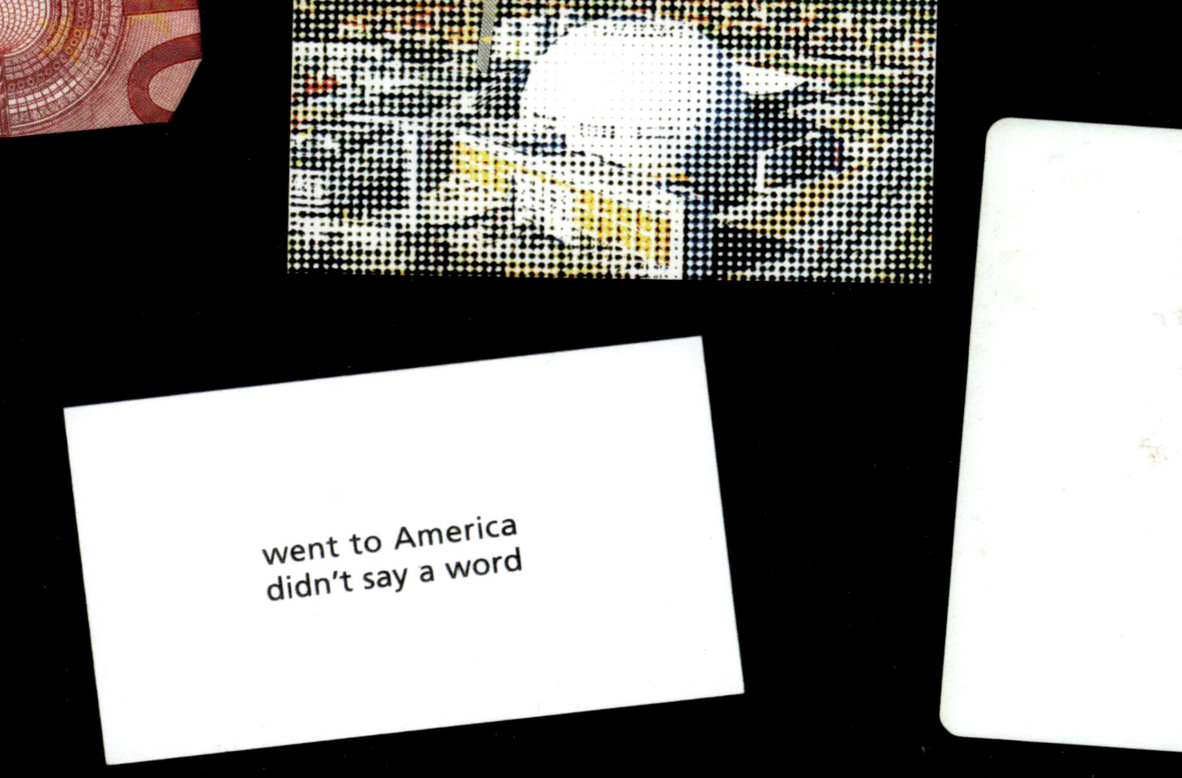
went to America
didn't say a word

Madame
Vera
Resident Psychic

Stanley Hotel
333 Wonderview
Estes Park , CO 80517

P.O. Box 2595
Estes Park , CO 80517

or by

appointment

(970) 586-8810

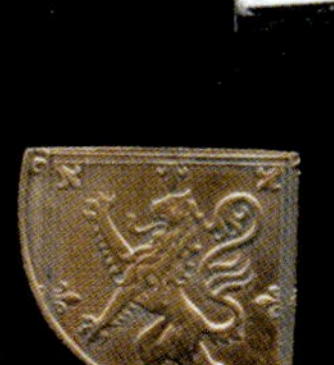
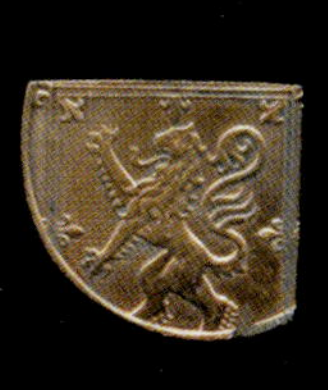
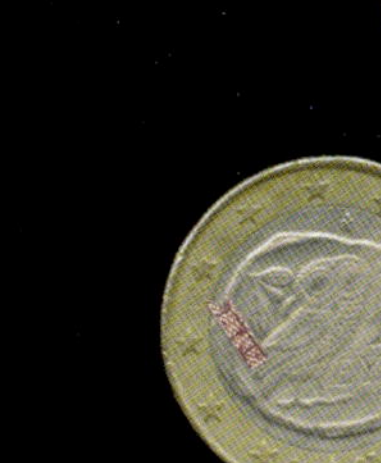
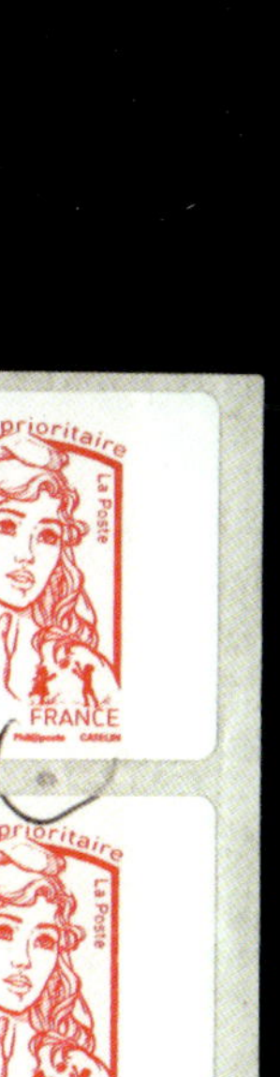
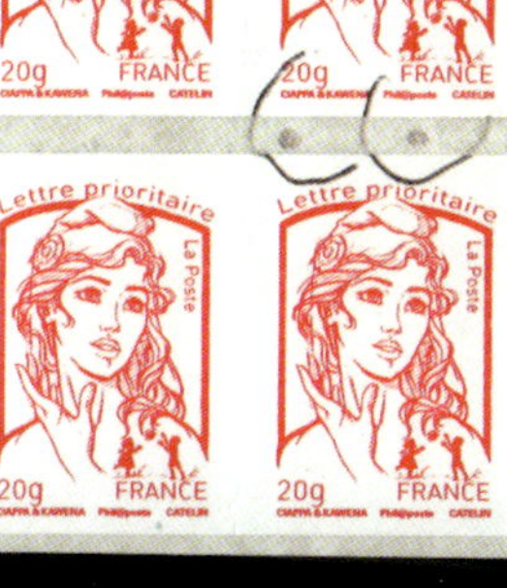

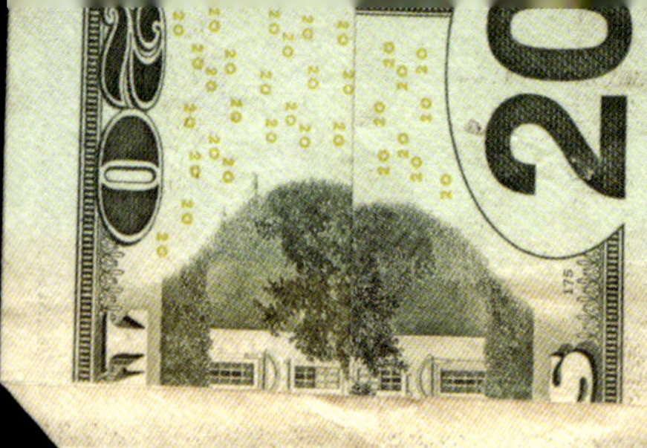

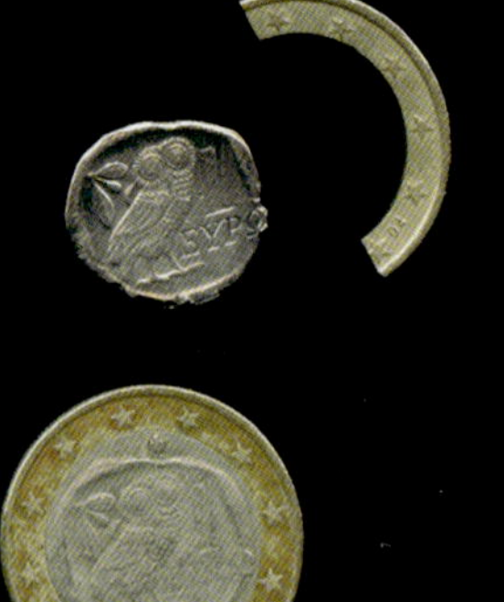

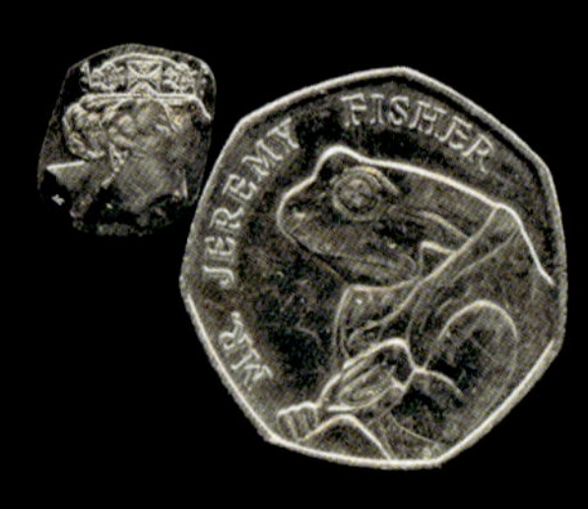

Adobe Photoshop

This application does not support the editing of banknote images.

For more information, select the information button below for Internet-based information on restrictions for copying and distributing banknote images or go to www.rulesforuse.org.

Cancel   Information

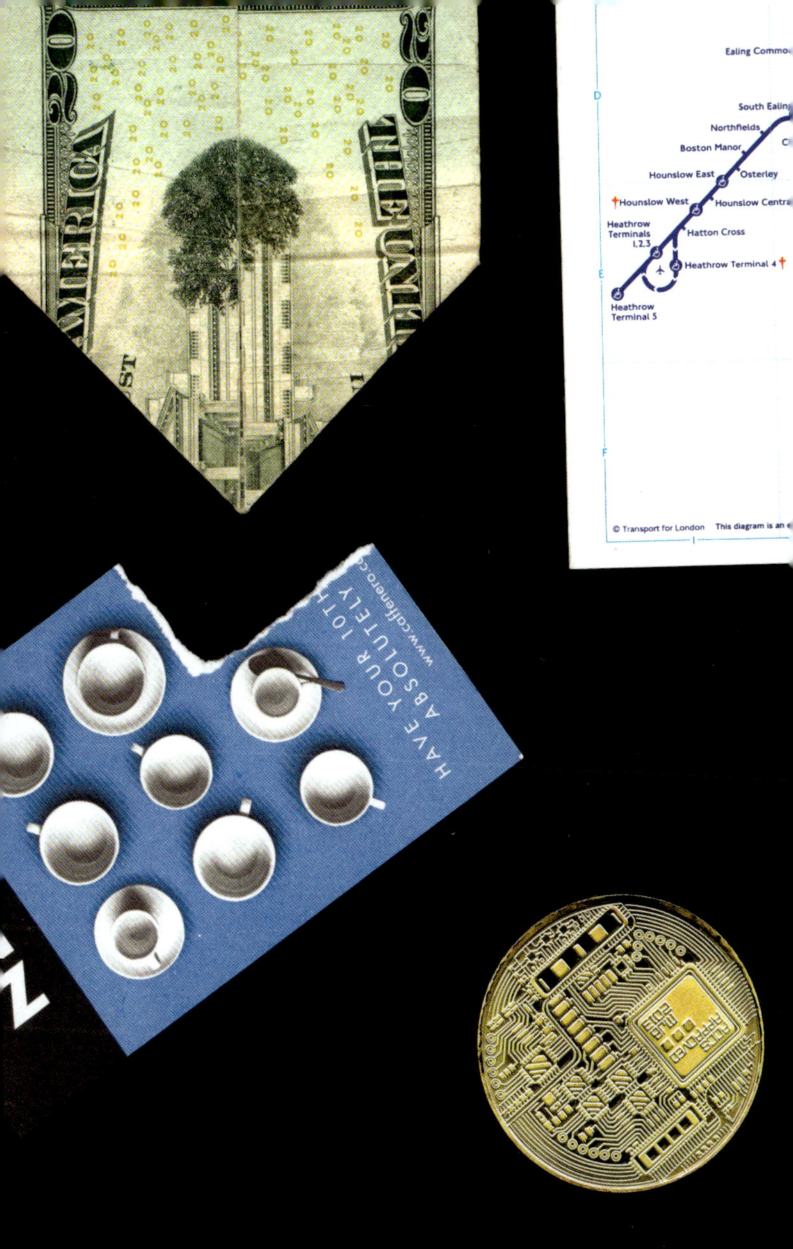
Ealing Common
South Ealing
Northfields
Boston Manor
Hounslow East
Osterley
Hounslow West
Hounslow Central
Heathrow
Terminals
1, 2, 3
Hatton Cross
Heathrow Terminal 4
Heathrow
Terminal 5
© Transport for London   This diagram is an e
HAVE YOUR ABSOLUTELY 10TH
www.cafferene.c
AMERICA
THE UNI
20

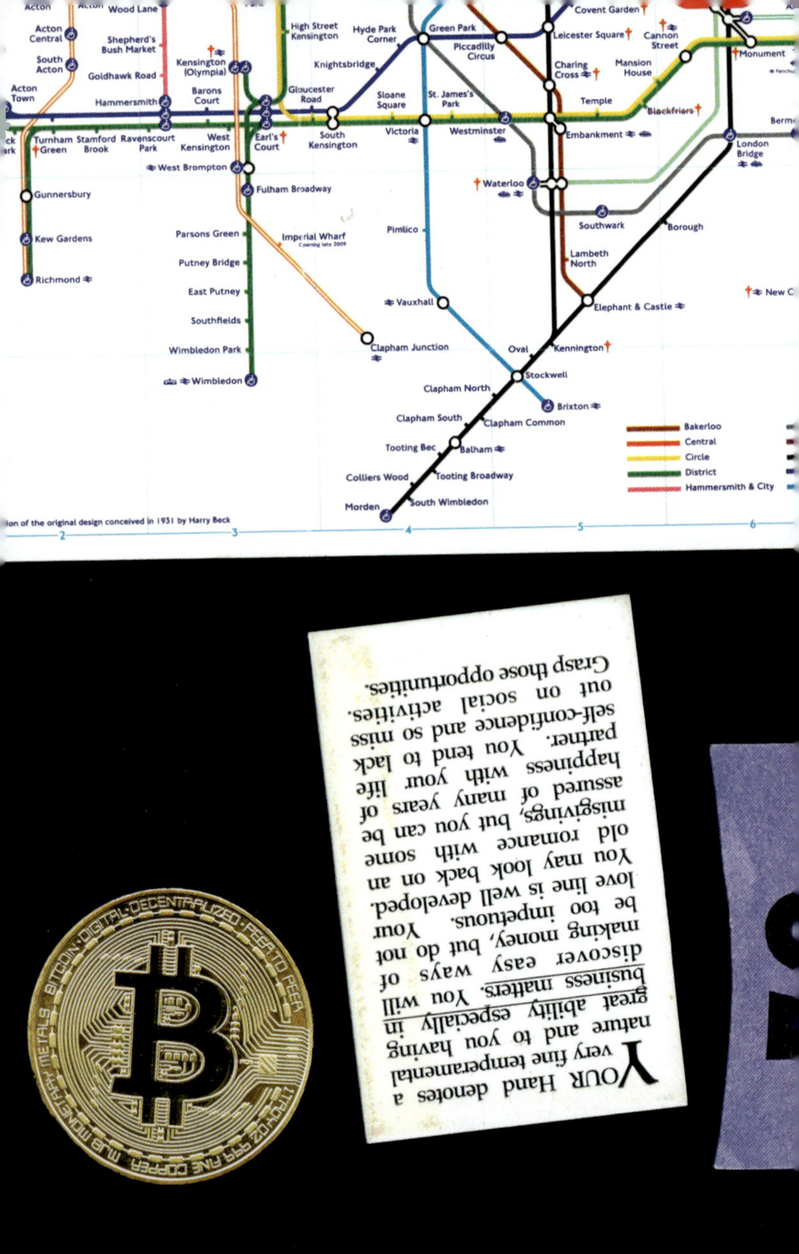

Acton · Acton · Wood Lane
Acton Central · Shepherd's Bush Market · High Street Kensington · Hyde Park Corner · Green Park · Covent Garden · Leicester Square · Cannon Street
South Acton · Goldhawk Road · Kensington (Olympia) · Knightsbridge · Piccadilly Circus · Charing Cross · Mansion House · Monument
Acton Town · Hammersmith · Barons Court · Gloucester Road · Sloane Square · St. James's Park · Temple · Blackfriars · Berm
Turnham Green · Stamford Brook · Ravenscourt Park · West Kensington · Earl's Court · South Kensington · Victoria · Westminster · Embankment · London Bridge
West Brompton
Gunnersbury · Fulham Broadway · Waterloo · Southwark · Borough
Kew Gardens · Parsons Green · Imperial Wharf (Opening late 2009) · Pimlico · Lambeth North
Richmond · Putney Bridge · Vauxhall · Elephant & Castle · New C
East Putney · Clapham Junction · Oval · Kennington
Southfields · Stockwell
Wimbledon Park · Clapham North · Brixton
Wimbledon · Clapham South · Clapham Common
Tooting Bec · Balham
Colliers Wood · Tooting Broadway
Morden · South Wimbledon

— Bakerloo
— Central
— Circle
— District
— Hammersmith & City

...ion of the original design conceived in 1931 by Harry Beck
2   3   4   5   6

DIGITAL · DECENTRALIZED · PEER TO PEER · BITCOIN · METALS · MLB MONETARY · FINE COPPER

Your Hand denotes a very fine temperamental nature and to you having great ability especially in business matters. You will discover easy ways of making money, but do not be too impetuous. Your love line is well developed. You may look back on an old romance with some misgivings, but you can be assured of many years of happiness with your life partner. You tend to lack self-confidence and so miss out on social activities. Grasp those opportunities.

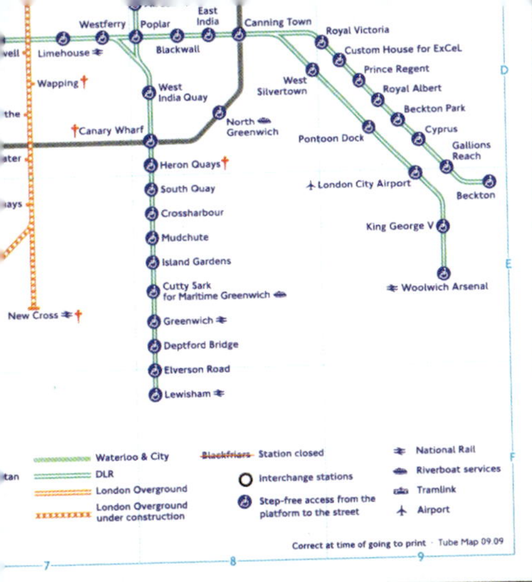

Westferry
Poplar
East India
Canning Town
Royal Victoria
vell
Limehouse
Blackwall
Custom House for ExCeL
Prince Regent
D
Wapping
West India Quay
West Silvertown
Royal Albert
the
Beckton Park
Canary Wharf
North Greenwich
Cyprus
Pontoon Dock
Gallions Reach
ays
Heron Quays
South Quay
London City Airport
Beckton
Crossharbour
Mudchute
King George V
E
Island Gardens
Cutty Sark
for Maritime Greenwich
Woolwich Arsenal
New Cross
Greenwich
Deptford Bridge
Elverson Road
Lewisham
Waterloo & City
Blackfriars Station closed
National Rail
tan
DLR
Interchange stations
Riverboat services
London Overground
Tramlink
London Overground under construction
Step-free access from the platform to the street
Airport
Correct at time of going to print · Tube Map 09.09
7
8
9
F

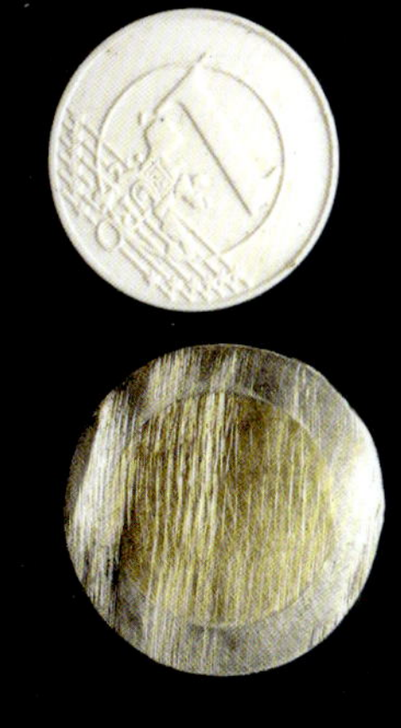

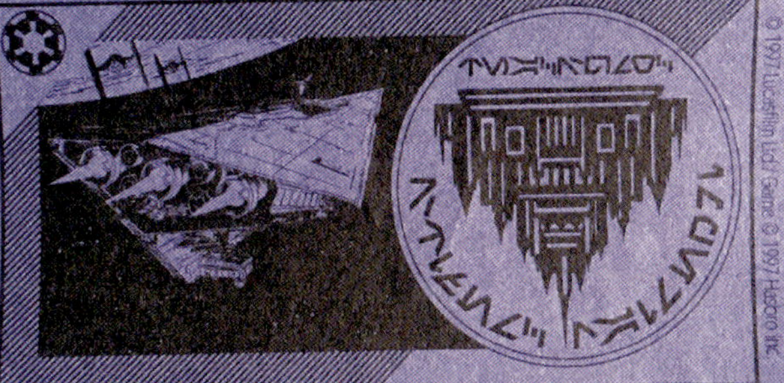

© 1997 Lucasfilm Ltd / Game © 1997 Hasbro Inc.

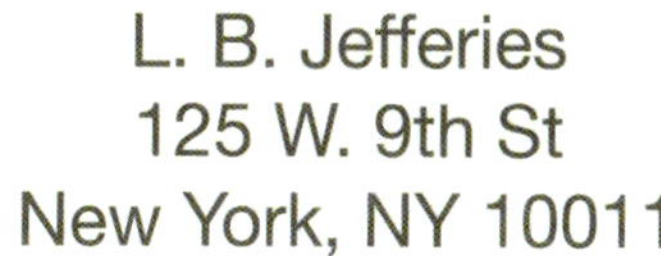

L. B. Jefferies
125 W. 9th St
New York, NY 10011

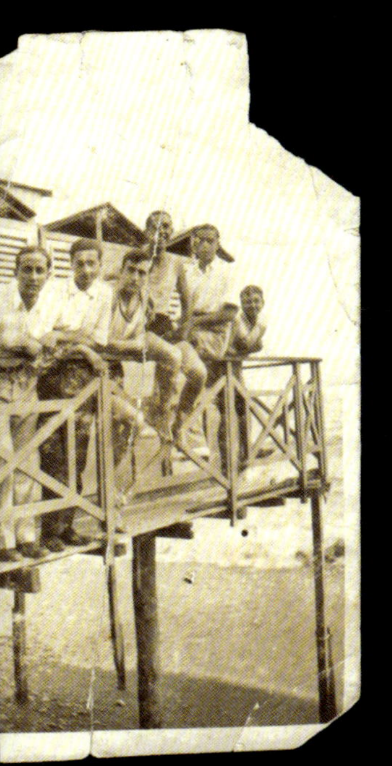

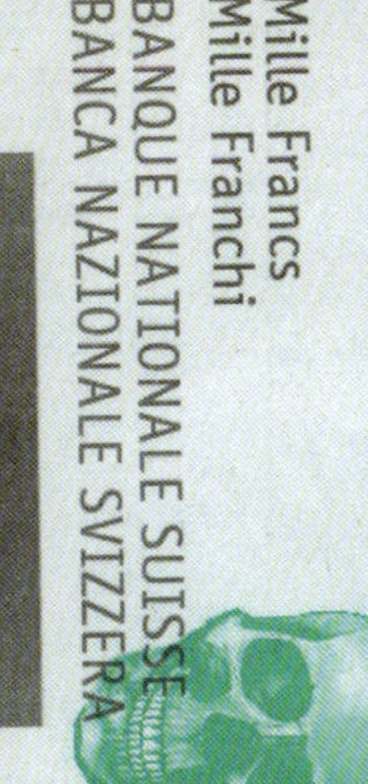

1000
Mille Francs
Mille Franchi
BANQUE NATIONALE SUISSE
BANCA NAZIONALE SVIZZERA
Or

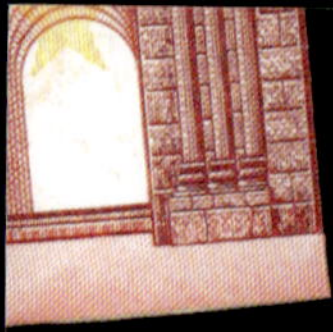

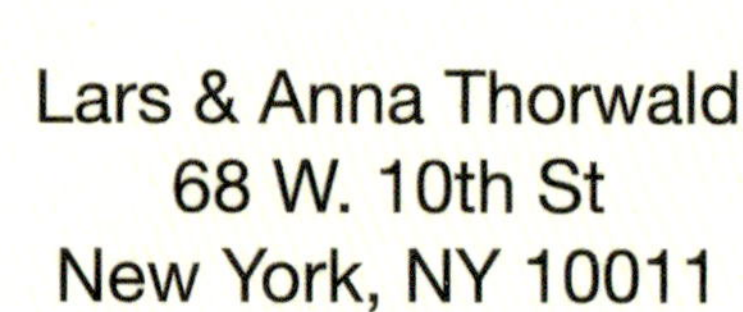

Lars & Anna Thorwald
68 W. 10th St
New York, NY 10011

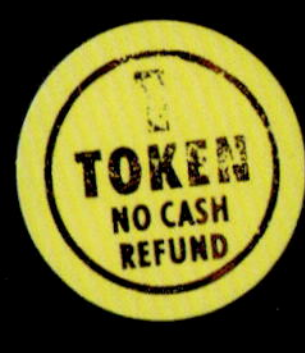

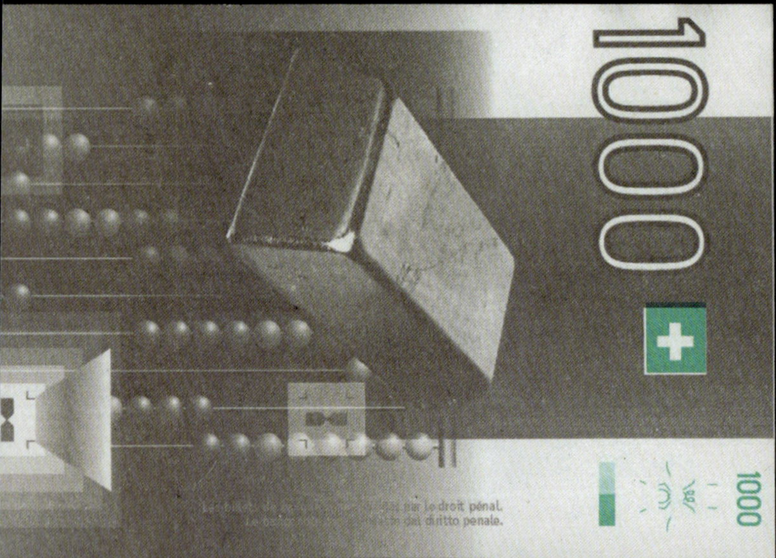

The Knife

Charlotte York

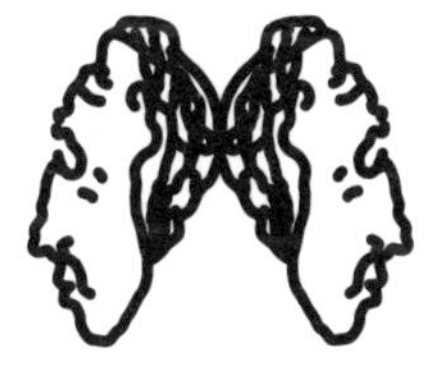

In the same collection:

The Knife, a guided tour since 2009
'All the Knives', 2012, an exhibition by Åbäke, Yaïr Barelli, Jochen
        Dehn, Dirk Elst, Aurélien Froment, Vladimir Ivaneanu, Sally
        O'Reilly, Matt Rogers and Adva Zakai with performers
        Oshin Albrecht, Adaline Anobile, Frédérique de
        Montblanc, Dana Dijkgraaf, Eveline Lambrechts, Lune
        Léoty, Michiel Reynaert, Rebecca Rosseel, Carlotta
        Scioldo, Barbara Van Beers, Suzy Vanderbiesen, Sanne
        Van Giel, Greet Verstraete, Gosie Vervloessem, Sofie
        Vrancken, Paola Zampierolo co-produced by Z33, Hasselt
        — Jan Boelen, Evelien Bracke — and Frans Masereel
        Centrum, Kasterlee — Sofie Dederen, Ivan Durt.
All The Knives, Any printed story on request, 2013, an exhibition
        catalogue published by Dent-de-Leone
The Knife, a silk scarf, 2014, produced with Mapoésie (Elsa Poux)
You are my Knife, a double-sided bomber jacket, 2019, produced
        with Peter Jensen and Gerard Wilson

The Knife, a book, 2020 is first published in an edition of 1989
        by Dent-de-Leone — 48 Wilton Way, London E8 1BG,
        United Kingdom, www.dentdeleone.com — written by
        Charlotte York, edited by Jonathan P. Watts, cover title
        by LPPL, designed by åbäke, set in Firenza; forewaord
        by Kajsa Ståhl; proofread by Gemma Holt; printed by Die
        Keure, Brugge; ISBN: 9781907908583

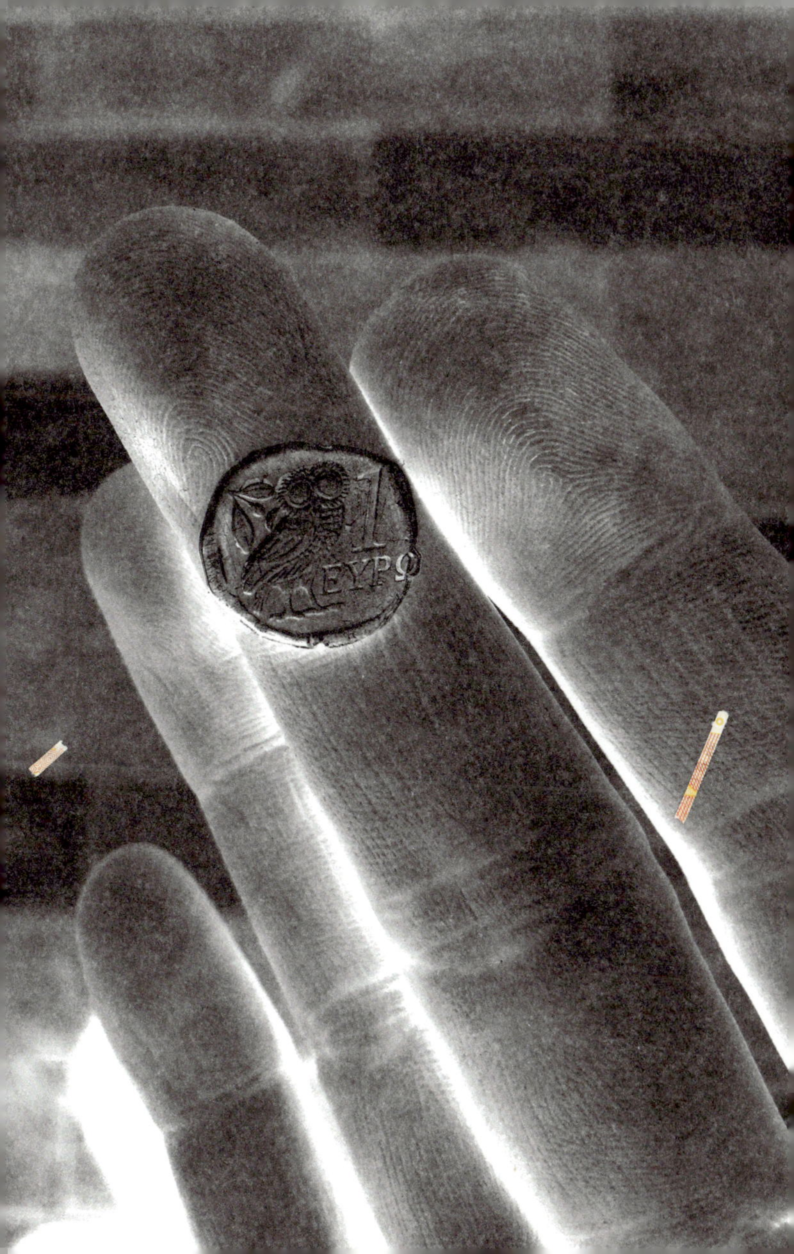

The Knife: It is only the beginning

I am your knife
All the knives
Table knife
Pocket knife
Who's the knife?
School of keeping
Curious tour
Unclassifiable trust
Dusty house
Wallet belief
Authentic poetry
Wild interpretation
Experimental theatre
Hair that matters
Folded story
Invisible people
Weird micro cosmos
Holding on
Object from abroad
Hyperlinked adventure
Valuable trash
Travelling light
Heated currency
Awaken museum
Graveyard walk
Family therapy

Retrieved knowledge
Wonderful relevance
Time returned
Credibility of the heart
Fairly uncertain at times
True knots
Blissful snap
Prostitution next door
Listening skills
Important photocopy
Knowingly existing
Sweet drug
& other waiting marvels.

—Kajsa of Åbäke

PS: It says that a knife is humankind's first weapon,
but words are the sharpest of them all. Having
been standing next to the author of this book
for the birth of most of these stories, often not
understanding the importance of keeping hold of
a found object for many, many years, travelling
across the seas, and even divorcing because of
it, now I finally understand. You should read this
book: it includes tales of personal importance.
I love it.

<h1 style="text-align:center">A note
that was handed to me by a ghost</h1>

The note is handwritten in pencil on a piece of thin textured paper that has been folded three times to approximately the size of a postcard: 'Do you know there was a female emperor in Chinese history? Do you know her name?' There is no inscription on the back.

I never like to visit art exhibitions with other people. Their pace intrudes upon mine and I constantly pay too much attention to how much time they spend in front of a painting or, even worse, a looped video. Will they think I'm shallow if I linger for too little time?

As a child I once looked at a Van Gogh painting for an hour just to prove to my schoolfriend that I was a real art fan when really I was just a fraud. As an adult I've come to appreciate art more personally but I unfortunately experience the judgmental gaze when accompanied by another.

Nowadays, my exhibition-going must happen on my own not just because of any concern to display my aesthetic erudition, but also because I don't want my companion to make a similarly laborious effort for me. Beyond this mild neurosis and character flaw, visiting exhibitions alone can excite intense encounters, especially performance works that are supposed to be for a larger audience. To be alone with a performer can either break the fourth wall and create embarrassment or be simply magical or both.

I was given this note by an Asian woman performing in a public art centre in Malmö, Sweden. I had to climb into the gallery and a further structure through a hole that was knocked into a plasterboard wall, probably with a sledgehammer, and, despite other visitors being present in the centre, I was on my own in the small cabin that was lit in ultraviolet neon. I recall a multitude of objects scattered and hanging even if the artist's name eludes me.

There was no sound but the lights flickered and the objects seemed to move slightly, including a white mass in the corner of my view, which suddenly appeared very close to me and instantly destroyed my composure as the exhibition audience. My body covered in goosebumps, I gasped and a hot prickly sensation swept across my back.

The white mass was not ugly but her white teeth and white face covered in make-up made her resemble a movie version of a ghost, particularly of the kind in Asian movies of the late 90s, except she had short disorderly hair.

I was shocked by her apparition but also because she stood so close to me I could smell her breath — that

intimate scent of the inside of someone. The smell
was not bad or minted or anything one would associate with a mouth, it was just intimate, a smell you
know of your siblings, lover or child. This disturbed
me greatly and it was exacerbated because I was on
my own.

Then she pulled a note from her pocket and smiled
at me. She asked — or did she just rhetorically recite
it? — 'Did you know there was a female emperor
in Chinese History? Do you know her name?' Then,
clearly off the score, she asked: 'Are you Chinese?'

Usually Asian people are very good at spotting the
different nationalities from the South East Asian regions. I was surprised at this because I'm only ever
asked if I'm Japanese or Mongolian. I relayed this to
her, that I was Japanese and surprised by her guess, to
which she replied: 'Oh, but Japanese people are slim.'

Money for sale

I often visit secondhand shops as they're the last remnants of accidental discovery when it comes to shopping. 'People who bought this also bought that,' is not the usual recommendation from the staff, whose job is mostly to receive and sort donated objects, objects donated by potential customers. Secondhand shops are often also the receptacle of handmade objects, such as paintings, ceramics or sculptures. It's intriguing who donates the stuff and even more so who buys it.

The American artist Jim Shaw has a big collection of thrift store paintings. Eventually he stopped buying any showing a face or hands because they were too easily strange and eerie. Apparently amateur and semi-professional painters mess up hands, faces and body proportions almost every time. It is, however, a wonderful feeling to rummage in a box of miscellaneous items that people believe could have a second or third life in a different home. Someone's former treasure is the next person's future rubbish.

It was in such a shop that I came across this banknote, pinned to the wall behind the shopkeeper. At first I thought it was an example of a fake, displayed as a warning that they knew how fake money looked should someone get the idea they could launder £10 batches in east London's secondhand shops.

On closer inspection the note was hand drawn in colour pencils and although it clearly depicted Darwin and a humming bird, it was difficult to say whether the craft was brilliant or simply crap. How could the counterfeiter think it would fool anybody? The paper was the right size yet the feel was completely wrong. I asked to see it and was wonderfully surprised that it even displayed a metallic dotted line, a security measure of the Bank of England rendered here in metallic felt-tip pen.

It was evidently the worst fake I'd seen, especially considering the time it would have taken for the forgery artist to draw it. Could it have been worth the labour? I enquired as to its origin and dared to ask if I could buy it. The shopkeeper didn't know who made it but agreed to sell it. My brain was torn as to what I was buying. Will it be cheap fake money or an expensive artwork? As I asked for its price the shopkeeper rolled her eyes and, as if I was truly dumb for asking said, 'Well, obviously £10.' To which, showing the reverse, left blank by a tired artist who probably moved on to something else, I replied, 'Shouldn't it be half of that?'

Reasoning forgery

Frans Masereel Centrum is a centre dedicated to graphic arts and all its possible digressions. It is located in Kasterlee, Belgium and a quick internet search would show the buildings that constitute the compound — a large blue-grey three-storey UFO surrounded by Californian A-frame houses (A-frame houses make me think of the Californian sun, best lemons and citrus — a far cry from the Belgian countryside, recalling the yellow of fries which aren't French).

The UFO building houses a wide range of printing facilities, beginning with the earliest techniques even before Gutenberg, and it all works thanks to the highly passionate members of staff that maintain them and provide technical and conceptual advice to their users. From acid etching to letterpress, screen printing to offset printing, Riso to laser engraving, it's all there.

The A-frame houses are used by residents who spend up to six weeks there, isolated with their own thoughts and the printing machines. Horses run in the neighbour's field and the centre's cockerels wake you in the morning.

It's in this idyllic place that the idea of making fake money came up.Six of us decided to draw each colour of the said banknote onto stone. Separating the colours by eye is not an easy affair, albeit a simple task for photoshop (I once lost a contest of mixing and matching colour at college, mistaking a maroon for a pink, ending a career in hyperrealistic painting). It was a failure. Forgery for profit had been proven to be a hopeless affair and the manufacturing of currency as a general scam is best left to the state.

Anyhow, at Frans Masereel we rediscovered the beauty of lithography, where drawing directly on a stone and based on the immiscibility of oil and water made it possible to print in numbers as accurately as anything the hand could draw on said stone.

Forgery as art also, it turns out, has a beautiful currency in the history of beautiful losers. The result of our work — made laboriously by overprinting the eye-separated hand-drawn colours — was one hundred banknotes of £10. Each one costs more than five times its face value to produce. The police would be puzzled and you would not need to be an expert to see the easy differences between ours and the official notes.

At the time of printing this text the notes are in slow circulation among people who would collect them without knowing exactly where they were from as no signature would exist except this very testimony.

The lies that bind

Euro banknotes were put into circulation in the beginning of the twenty-first century. They somehow signify the European Union or make it clear that one aspect is an economical and financial union. In Europe we can buy stuff with the same money!

It is rather rare to see a €500 banknote, which is more or less the equivalent of 500 baguettes (for the French), 500 espresso coffees (for the Italians) or 100 beers (for the Czech) or 100 Pretzels (for the Germans) at the turn of the century. Everything quickly became more expensive. A unique monetary system for such a diverse groupings of countries. The design is colourful. Each note shows on one side a gate and on the other a bridge. This is obviously a metaphor for the construction of a bigger state: yes, open that door and come in, cross the bridge and we'll be together.

The design meeting must have been fun, especially because each of those architectural achievements are specifically drawn to evoke an existing door, gate or bridge while never being a specific one. You will not recognise the aqueduct of Segovia from Spain or the iron bridge from Riga because the EU feared it would result in conflict between the 19 countries.

This makes sense as you wouldn't want paper money to be the source of discord between people who want to get back to how it was before the Tower of Babel or something. What is surprising to me is the beautiful compromise about such a decision, visible to all the citizens of the European Union everyday: this big union won't be easy. So difficult in fact that even though there are hundreds, perhaps thousands, of architectural masterpieces of bridges and gates within the European Union, one had to commission an illustrator to make sure none of the bridges would be recognisable to a zealous nationalist.

One could argue that they could have gone for animals or plants, provoking anthropocentric debates as to whether a specific flower is more Dutch or Italian. Since it is strangely customary to represent people on banknotes one can only dream of a big meeting to decide whose bust, among the rich and long history of 19 different countries, should adorn the only seven spots. Perhaps they should also be composites? For instance, someone between Charlotte Perriand, Rainer Werner Fassbinder, Copernicus and Amália Rodrigues.

Another composite would be the perfect European, combining all the stereotypes, genders, immigration histories, past, present and future, a wonderful human with all the intellectual and physical qualities, the ultimate person, full of compassion yet with their flaws and the fragility of the human condition. I guess that person could be on all the notes from different angles and ages, €5 would show its little head coming out of its mum and the €500 the very exact and precise moment of a peaceful death after 120 years of a rewardingly exciting life.

Folded
Stockhausen $20 bill

America is the land of freedom, America is the land of opportunity, America is great — again?

As a young country America has made enormous an impact since it was so-called 'discovered' by the Europeans, a bold claim considering one can assert that it was certainly populated before Christopher Columbus or Erik the Viking set foot on a whole continent (conspiracy theories and official Histories concur and collapse into one).

If you start to fold a $20 banknote the way one would to make an airplane (a Boeing 767, perhaps) you can create a new illustration which allegedly shows the twin towers of the World Trade Center — also a bold statement — designed by American architect Minoru Yamasaki, on fire, just before their collapse during the September 11, 2001 attacks by Al-Qaeda terrorists.

If we consider that the bills were designed a long time prior to the attacks and even long before the birth of the terrorist organisation, it is rather prescient. Such post-rationalisation is disturbing but not very surprising. What does it suggest? That America, or some of its powerful leaders had planted a clue relating to one of the most important historical events of the twenty-first century in plain sight on one of the most circulated printed matter in the country? Was it a warning for people who tried to prevent it — an all-American Nostradamus gesture — or just a sinister easter egg by the egomaniac culprits?

Everybody seems to remember where they were and what they were doing on that day. In our studio in London it was a day like any other and believe it or not we were listening to the radio rather than following the tragedy on the internet. We continued to go about our affairs and in the evening made our way to a lecture by the graphic designer Stefan Sagmeister who lived and worked in New York. On arrival to the venue we were told the talk was cancelled due to the terrorist attacks occurring that day. Everybody's mood was somber and the discussions and speculations were all centred on the plane crashes. To escape it all we went to the pub and after a few pints joined some friends at a bar in Hoxton. One drink led to another and the next thing we know we are six people in an otherwise empty club dancing until the early hours of the next day.

What came over us? What madness made us be oblivious to the fact the rest of London had probably gone home to quietly be with their families and reflect on the preciousness of life, the fragility of the world order and how small a human being is. Seventeen years after the events I am still unsure of my own feelings about our bizarre reaction. Coincidentally or not we never saw the friends we went dancing with again.

PS: Are you also disturbed by the fact 9/11, as the event is colloquially called, is also the number for the emergency services as it has been since 1968, more than 30 years before the attacks? Probably not.

A smiling Gandhi is on every banknote in India — the equivalent of Queen Elizabeth II in the UK. The graphic elements of a banknote are a small statement of affirmation and I often wonder just how important these people are to the nation.

It seems normal to us that money is graphically associated with a person or a landmark when really the links are often tenuous. Usually the person is dead before being used as a national symbol, creating, at times, interesting paradoxes, such as Andrew Jackson on the $20 bill. Jackson, the seventh president of the United States in the early nineteenth century, was not only suspicious towards paper money but opposed to a central bank.

Some decision-making people have a sense of irony. While Gandhi never professed anything against money specifically, the sanctified figure doesn't fit so well with the materialism accompanying cash as he criticised both capitalism and communism for focusing on materialistic views of humans, unless we take into account that there is a discrepancy between the saint we all seem to know and a much more complex and human Gandhi. Which reminds me of an American friend of mine who happens to be a creationist. This friend is a brilliant artist but he's obviously crazy —

go figure. I myself believe there's very little evidence for creationism and, yes, they can be scary fanatics but this guy is my friend so that's that.

The first time he came to visit me in Britain I pointed out the fact that the £10 banknote showed Darwin and that this was funny considering he was a denier of the theory of evolution. My friend and I had a lot of fun discussing how bizarre it was that the Old Testament didn't mention dinosaurs if, as he believes, Earth was just 6000 years old. In response, he would say that Marco Polo never mentioned the Great Wall of China despite visiting the country's four corners and more. I suppose he couldn't envisage that Polo might have invented some of his stories.

Anyway, I did challenge him to never handle the Darwin £10 as it would align him with contrary beliefs and was surprised when in principle he agreed. Later that day I witnessed him refuse to take a Darwin banknote at a supermarket and argue about it with the cashier and the manager. The conversation was absurd and amused fellow shoppers for a while. For me it was simply beautiful, especially as the discussion shifted towards abstract philosophical views between the verbal jousters, having forgotten it started with money.

This was a few years ago and my friend who has visited Britain regularly since has never once accepted to use the Darwin banknote. To see him enter a bank to exchange the note issued from the ATM is something I will miss now that the father of evolution has been replaced by Jane Austen — although my friend did once tell me he doesn't like her writings.

A card showing
Mount Rushmore on one side
and Crazy Horse memorial on the other

In European hostels you sometimes find a rotating display of business card-sized flyers about all the tourist attractions in the area. Let's say you're in Amsterdam in a touristic hotel, just before breakfast, waiting for your companion who is still in the shower while you've been awake since 6 am, not daring to go out because it's your first time in Europe. You're standing in front of a carousel of business card-sized flyers, all perforated so they hang and display a colourful palette of the Sex Museum, the Bag Museum, the Stedelijk Museum, the Van Gogh Museum, etc.

They're all neatly designed in a uniform fashion and provide the necessary information for a wide range of activities and places. As the cards erase all differences between the attractions there are very few indications of what is an old respectable public institution or a borderline scam. Everything is on the same level. I don't know anybody that would use these cards as their primary source of information on how to spend time in a place they know nothing about. On the other hand, they might be for the disorganised, the possibly adventurous ones or the trustful ones who, like me, believe that anything printed is authoritative information.

When my family and I crossed North America on the obligatory road trip — anyone with a chance to do so truly should take it — we had to see Mount Rushmore in South Dakota, primarily because of Alfred Hitchcock's film *North by North West* (1959). Was I expecting to run on top of Lincoln's head? Slide down Roosevelt's nose and hang there like a European bogey?

As europeans, it was astonishing to us all to see such a monument as there are no comparable endeavours in Europe. Don't get me wrong, big headed monarchs, politicians and crazy projects are legion, from fantastic castles to capricious assertion of power through architecture. The dubious monuments are today the delight of tourists. But the big face of a chief of state the size of a mountain is of another order.

Megalomaniac despots could do such things although neither Ceauşescu nor Stalin dared disfigure nature to replace it with their own scaled-up visage. Only in America, one would be tempted to say in front of such puzzling effort. Then again, America has its Superman while we only have the likes of Arsène Lupin or Miss Marple, fantastic heroes but incapable of flying.

Mount Rushmore is highly secured and one must view it on the specially-designed viewing platform from the visitor centre. There is no wilderness: even the rubble at the base of Rushmore looks perfectly placed, a museum within which they walled a mountain with the sky as its ceiling.

It wasn't as perfect when they started the project. Jefferson's face was on the left before they realised, after half the face had been carved, that it would not be possible to finish. What a beautiful repentance it would have been to leave this trace of the fragility of humans — a reminder that all art is uncertain, a little dirty on the edge before it is varnished and hung on immaculate white walls.

Less than half an hour drive away is the Crazy Horse memorial, which is similar to Mount Rushmore in that it depicts another war leader. To compare the two helped me understand why there is no natural inclination in the United States to implement social security and why President Obama struggled so much to create some of it when this seems so evident to us in Europe. Let me explain.

The Crazy Horse memorial is effectively the vision and work of a single man as opposed to Rushmore, a state project. Crazy Horse fought the invading forces that are still in power today, having won, over time, legitimacy, albeit challenged. The White Men are in power and represent the system, or to abbreviate it: The Man. Some Americans are suspicious of the federal government. Accepting grants seems to them the same as giving up the belief that any person can achieve anything or is allowed to try on their own American-basic-right-merit. Hence, the carving of a leader of a minority into a mountain was born from the dream of a single Polish immigrant in the beginning of the twentieth century. Even when federal money was offered on several occasions it was refused.

Currently there is only a face but the unformed rock face will be developed into the full body of the chief riding a horse, dwarfing the four presidents on the nearby mountain. There's no deadline as to when it will be completed but it doesn't stop the Crazy Horse being visited. Money collected from visitors is the main income to secure bulldozers and explosives, the chisels of this upscaled sculpture. One can see a heroic and strange logic to this defiance towards power, and, perhaps, but this is just my naive inter-pretation, explains that agreeing that the state takes care of the feeble and the weak by having a social security system is difficult to accept.

Heart and kidneys
and cornea and lungs donor cards

In Great Britain donor cards are often kept in the wallet. On one side of the card a red, stylised valentine heart is suspended in the middle of a blue background bordered by white. As well as representing one of the possible donations, the heart symbolises the fact that the carrier possesses kindness of heart to gift, post-mortem, parts of themself to a total stranger. The other side of the card is a list of body parts with accompanying tick boxes. One might choose only to donate the lungs or cornea, or by ticking another box the whole body (are there parts of the body that are useless?). There is a space to write one's name and another for a signature.

How simple this is. I imagine a traffic accident that leaves me lying face down on the road, my last thoughts why that morning, and for the first time in my life, I wore my underwear back to front, being too lazy to change, and now some medics will see this and laugh at this clumsiness, imagining that my whole life was lived in such squalor, that I forgot about appointments and was constantly day-dreaming, never achieving anything at all, when what really happened was that I thought it was interestingly comfortable and wondered whether there was a design question differentiating the front and the back. (Make no mistake: I know there are biological differences but in this case I perhaps came to understand I'd always bought boxer shorts a size or two bigger, making the central pouch at the front as insignificant as the split panels at the rear.)

Anyway, the medics would see my wallet, wonder what all that junk was, and finally find my donor card, double check the name, possibly the signature, before opening my chest in the ambulance to detach the still-warm heart. 'He had a big heart,' the medic would say, before storing it in a cooler box. We would arrive in the hospital where a French woman named Peggy Mathis would already be lying on the operating table. The surgeon would immediately transplant the quivering heart of mine into her chest and with the miracle of science she would live a beautiful life ever after, never knowing that back in our childhood I was secretly in love with her but never dared to tell.

Burn
my money

In the Vietnamese supermarkets of east London there's always a corner dedicated to funeral items. Typically, they consist of actual size paper reproductions of shoes, shirts, mobile phones or money, items that are burnt during funerals in South East Asia. For £1.99 you can get a bundle of $100 bills.

Once our design collective exhibited such an item half burnt in an installation at a gallery in San Francisco. I suppose it was too tempting to send an artwork of fake dollar bills through US Customs, having to fill in a form of its perceived value and showing this burnt American god in a vitrine.

There was no budget to fly us out so we just hoped the install went well, that drinks were had at the opening, and that some visitors would find the show life-changing. A while later we received a forwarded email in which the curator, Jon Sueda, was speaking to the director of the institution in a panic as our exhibit had been stolen despite the vitrine being secured. The exchange had a desperate tone and it was obvious from the way they spoke to each other that we'd been copied in by mistake.

We were bemused by this although we felt for Jon's concerns. What if we pressed charges? What if we asked for compensation that was far above any budget they did not have? What if we asked for the head of either or both of them to be sent on a silver plate across the Atlantic to adorn our studio as a trophy? We replied immediately to quell the suspense and to reassure them that neither the director nor Jon would be required to chop their small fingers off as a token of their unacceptable failure.

Instead, we asked them to re-enact the theft and give us the footage. As for the exhibit, we asked that they file for theft, request the police go through the procedure of dusting for fingerprints on the vitrine glass, then place the report in the vitrine in place of the work, effectively becoming the work. All of this Jon carried out.

Sometimes I think about whoever stole the banknotes. The bills are so badly printed on poor paper (albeit perfect for burning) that it is difficult to understand how they were mistaken for real money. Actually, $100 bills are less common than $20 bills and perhaps they weren't as familiar with the way they look. Unless, and this would be quite extraordinary, they were stolen as artworks, which is unlikely because none of the other sculptures in the vitrines were stolen and they were far more valuable. Had any of those been stolen because of security lapses we would, indeed, have asked for Jon's head.

There is higher to the highest

As a child I remember my parents gasping in front of the television at a man burning a banknote. I had no idea why he was doing so, nor why my parents were so shocked, although their smiles suggested the awe was mixed with admiration. At the time, any pocket money I received was given in coins so a banknote immediately felt as though it belonged to the adult world. All I knew was that it was a waste — just think of how many sweets would be lost to flames. Later, as a grown up, I understood that this gesture had been famously made by the shocking musical genius Serge Gainsbourg on primetime TV.

At the time there were few TV channels, which guaranteed that most French people actually saw the act. In the midst of an interview Gainsbourg was asked about how rich he was. Irritated by this question, he took out a 500 franc note, the biggest at the time, and a lighter. The interviewer warned him: 'You know what you're about to do is illegal, right?' To which Serge replied, 'Yes', and lit the note, continuing: 'I'll show you what is left for me after tax.' The singer-song-writer put out the flames when only a little corner of the note remained between his thumb and finger. This seminal moment in television was followed by millions of people.

Some time later, I read, the same Serge Gainsbourg was seated in a Parisian cafe when he recognised Francis Bacon on the terrace. He stood and went to the painter to ask for an autograph on a banknote — this one I believe was not the one he burned live on TV.

I was at an opening reception at the V&A Museum in London when I caught a glimpse of the ever so slightly awkward interaction between two people when one asks an autograph from the other. The deference and sometimes humiliation is a very particular emotion I often push myself to feel (Tracey Emin, why did you refuse me and leave me standing on the street while you looked at me with pity and anger?).

On this occasion I almost ran towards the two men and quickly equipped myself with a piece of paper and pen, intruding the two men's space. The man who received the autograph was satisfied and the one who gave it glowed with pride, somehow. I then asked the man who got the autograph to sign one for me. The person who was apparently famous said: 'Is this a joke?' to which I replied, 'Well, don't you know him?' He is Bob and Roberta Smith, the famous contemporary artist. As I said this I scrutinised the face of the interjecting person and concluded I did not know who he was.

A torn $1 bill I may have stolen

Hans-Peter Feldmann is a German artist. In 2010 he won the prestigious Hugo Boss Prize for contemporary artists. The award is $100,000 and an exhibition at the Guggenheim in New York, which comes with its own production budget, of course. Feldman decided to link the two parts of the award by using his prize money as the raw material of the exhibition. If a $1 bill measures 156.1 x 66.3mm, a surface area of 10349.43mm^2, then 100,000 of them is enough to cover the entire galleries in which Feldman was invited to exhibit. It was funny and clever, and, in theory, the artwork would go back to being monetary currency at the end of the show. There was $100,000 at the beginning, then a big exhibition, then $100,000 in the end — minus, that is, all the notes stolen by the smartypants visitors.

While Hans-Peter Feldmann's art is often witty and humorous it is also, if one takes the time to engage with it, very deeply affecting. One standout work of his is an unlimited edition of $1 bills on which each Washington has its nose painted over in red. What could this mean?

Several friends of mine own the work, which is usually framed and exhibited on the wall. This edition cost $1050, a bargain for a piece of art and also a testament that art need faith to exist, especially in the face of buying money which has been defaced in a gesture that can possibly reveal the nature of the farce that commercial art can be. I often wonder whether one of these have ever been put back into circulation where its value would shift radically, and possibly be considered defaced and therefore nullified.

The common destiny of artworks using money is that they are taken out of the monetary value system to jump into another one, arguably more lucrative and speculative. The Brazilian artist Cildo Meireles used to write political messages on banknotes so they could be seen by many, just as Suffragettes defaced coins and marked them with their demands.

A €10 note with a blind-embossed
sentence that reads: 'A group of people
standing outside of a closed day centre'

There I was at WIELS Contemporary Art Centre in Brussels in 2012, enjoying the exhibition 'Joy in People', a retrospective of the English artist Jeremy Deller, which included the recreation of his room where he organised his first show in 1993 while his parents were on holiday, as well as various unrealised projects, such as a live drawing session of a nude Iggy Pop (a project he would later realise).

One of the works consisted of three or four blind-embossing tools available on plinths for people to use. Blind embossing is achieved using a clamp that embosses a chosen image or text onto paper. It's still common to see old library books embossed with the name of the library on the title page. Embossing doesn't use ink but permanently marks the paper and, in theory, would work on any thin material that is flexible and rigid enough such as a leather jacket. It does't mark most textiles and breaks most dried leaves.

This work of Deller's was terribly inviting and I ended up stamping all the banknotes I had in my wallet: pounds, euros and a few dollars that for some reason I had. The embossed message is a thought-provoking way of sharing messages at a time when social media can multiply content with tremendous speed and efficacy. Two other embossing tools read the following: 'A Range Rover crushed and made into a bench' and 'Hell Is Other People's Money'.

I once lost my wallet on a train in France. In all probability it fell out of my back jean pocket while I was sleeping, but the suspicious person I am led me to conclude that it had definitely been stolen, and so off I went to the local police station where the following exchange occurred:

Me: 'Hello, my wallet has been stolen.'

Policeman: 'Okay, follow me and we'll fill in a form.'

I sit down and there's a computer screen between us on which he types the information I give him.

P: 'What is the value of the content? How much money was in there?'

M: 'Well, some coins, twenty euros and, I think, a dollar bill.

P: 'Anything else?'

M: 'The wallet is worth eighty pounds but more importantly there were artworks in it.'

P: 'Artwork, yes. What is the value of those?'

M: 'Five thousand euros.'

The rapid response was not so much based on my estimation of Jeremy Deller's work but the fact that it seemed essential to give it a monetary value for the interaction to make sense for the policeman. Indeed, what would be the point of reporting the theft of an object which, in my opinion, started as an artwork but now continues circulating in society outside of the white cube context — a little like the bicycle seat sculpture discarded as garbage and recycled by someone as a seat for their bicycle, as in Jean-Luc Godard's film *La Chinoise* (1967).

P: 'What kind of artwork was it?'

I can tell by his facial expression that he is scrolling a drop-down menu.

P: 'Sculpture or painting?'

Me: 'It's, erm, a conceptual artwork.'

P: 'What is that?'

Me: 'It is an artwork that starts with an idea, for example, this guy Jeremy Deller recently asked a group of people who were striking and rioting during the Thatcher years to re-enact the battles with the police the way enthusiasts reenact Napoleonic battles. This same artist displayed embossing machines at an exhibition so that whatever visitors embossed became an artwork.'

P: 'Yes, but I don't have this category.'

He chuckles a little. By then a connection had occurred between us and we laughed lightly at the deadend situation. He then said:

'We have a system that links all the police stations in France so our forms are the same. What I can do is send an official request to add this category to the drop-down menu.'

Me: 'Oh that would be great — there are many categories that are not only the medium used.'

We parted with a feeling of a small step accomplished and the next day I was called by a railway station manager who had found my wallet. Everything was in it.

A double-sided business card,
black print on one side and silver foil on the other

In Brett Easton-Ellis's 1991 novel *American Psycho* Patrick Bateman is a mid-1980s Manhattan investment banker and, like most of his colleagues, he is white, male, attractive, perfecting and relentless. Bateman, according to the confessional first-person narrative, is also a serial killer but unlike another character from a contemporary movie about serial killers, *Henry, portrait of a serial killer* (1986), he is a rich and successful yuppie from Wall street — not a lone, uneducated drifter as American serial killers tend to be portrayed.

Like many, I was fascinated by this postmodern novel that was both a diagnosis of the sickness of capitalism and consumerism, and the madness of how shallow and insignificant it all could be when a powerful man such as Patrick Bateman needed to justify his own existence by hacking into pieces prostitutes and colleagues. Reading it as a young adult was disturbing and I wasn't expecting to return to it when, later, I studied graphic design. It was one scene in particular that I half remembered.

At the time I was looking for evidence that graphic design existed in the general collective consciousness, that it was not just a strange job nobody had ever heard of. Often people knew a logo — perhaps they'd even drawn some themselves — but if you spoke of book layout it was obvious that most people wouldn't consider any of the choices involved in the production process to be a real job, in the way that being an architect or a nurse is. They may be right. Anyhow, one way to collect my 'evidence' was to compile movie clips — this was before YouTube and a Google search of 'graphic designers in mainstream media' would yield results — in which a character playing a graphic designer had to explain what the profession was. Inevitably, it was comical.

The movie version of *American Psycho* was released in 2000 and I remembered the business card scene where Bateman's insane thoughts are directed towards a business card of a colleague, far superior in design and quality to his, prompting disturbingly hilarious thoughts of murder mixed with a lyrical piece of critical writing that to this day is unrivalled in design writing.

I was disappointed by the movie and its depiction of the scene because I recalled it being so incredibly intense in the book. Perhaps it was because a book is usually read in silence and Bateman's neurosis as an internal voice echoes your own when reading it: you are the closest to a serial killer thinking of killing someone merely because their choice of typeface is better.

In Japan, where the business card is still a prevalent form of communication, people look at this piece of card with trust. It is the first encounter with you, before the smile or the clothes, before the scent or the *je ne sais quoi* of this shyness or overconfidence you exude. Inspecting a business card, feeling it with the tips of your fingers, being given the time to read it while facing a stranger who is doing the same thing is a rare ritual these days.

A contact card to the Cimitero
Monumentale di Staglieno, Naples

A cemetery typically will be the last domicile for all of us and for the living a ritualistic destination for one-way communication. One can visit them to pay respect to strangers or simply enjoy the quiet and reflexive space that such havens command. It was the phone number of the cemetery that appealed to me when I picked up a card for this place in Italy. It reminded me of an anecdote my friend Alexandra had told me.

The first concerned the alleged interest in mysticism by the man of technology Thomas Edison. Edison, of course, is one of the greatest inventors of our modern times and the pragmatism of this science giant and businessman is legendary. He was also, perhaps surprisingly, a believer of the world beyond death and worked on a device that would allow the living to communicate with the dead — think of it as a phone to the dead.

This was to prove a less successful invention than the phonograph or the light bulb. Although the trials of the invention are not well documented, it doesn't necessarily mean it didn't work. Sir Gilbert Scott, ar-chitect-designer of the iconic red K2 phone booth in the UK, may have had this in mind when he modelled his design proposal after the grave of John Soane.

Japanese filmmaker Hideo Nakata may have also had Edison's invention in mind when he directed Ring (1998) in which a deadly ghost curse is passed on through watching a VHS tape and a mute phone call.

Communication with the dead is what most people do when going to visit a grave, sometimes bringing flowers, recounting world events or giving news of the latest grandchild. I don't know anyone interred at the Cimitero Monumentale di Staglieno in Naples but, just like people leaving lipstick marks on Oscar Wilde's grave in Paris, I wanted to see the tomb of the Appiani family, of which I had no link nor prior knowledge of. This sculptural grave, however, is on the cover of Joy Division's second album, Closer. It came out after the lead singer Ian Curtis's suicide, although the cover had been designed before the tragedy. In my confused brain this actual tomb acquired a referential significance to an important English band leader's death. Going there was to pay tribute and respect to this post-punk hero who never set foot in Naples.

A business card stating I am a teacher at
Genève, Haute école d'art et de design

Almost immediately after graduation my peers and I
began teaching graphic design. The border between
these two worlds — teaching and being taught —
used to be much harder and the move from one to
the other would be a long, arduous path. Somehow
it wasn't so for us in our collective. Immediately I
was given the responsibility of leading the designers
of tomorrow towards an enlightened future of brilliance and academic success, not to mention a strong
independent practice. I was, myself, young and igno-
rant, still fresh from the protectorate of the student
fortress, unable to sustain myself and the collective I
belonged to and seriously questioning the relevance
of our work at large.

The advantage of teaching and the unavoidable hi-
erarchy sustained sometimes by the students themselves perhaps has something to do with the fact
that whatever claim or comment you make you must
apply to yourself. Be more radical! Do more research!
Contact the archbishop! This is advice you can give
if they apply to you too (I dread to think of teachers
who do not have a practice and therefore can swim
in the quiet waters of radical wisdom imparted to the
young ones without the safeguards of a reality check).

Anyone can teach in British design academia (I do it without the qualifications required of other European countries), although so often my colleagues and I have been kept from being on a payroll, which would perhaps be the evidence that we are only guest lecturers, even if this temporary status is highly dubious when it applies for seven years (twice I have been a 'guest' for seven years, in London and Geneva, totalling 14 years of 'visiting'). I'm not complaining about this. While the administration keeps you at arm's length, not having to pay you during school and college holidays, this fragile contract allows you to ignore administrative tasks, meetings with the devilish upper-management circles and, in recent years, the bookkeeping of scoring grants and preferring overseas customers to 'home' customers.

Anyhow, I had been pestering my employers for a business card for years. In Japan teaching is such a highly-regarded job that attitudes of people around you totally change and you become the wise living treasure professors are in this country — perhaps I wanted it for the privileges this would afford? Perhaps not. The sole aim to get this piece of card would be to get access to the discounted tariff in most museums in the world.

After years of being met with one excuse after another I just went ahead and made it myself using one of the online print-on-demand services (which, by the way, never ask for credentials so it would probably be okay to print anyone's card there). On receiving this fraudulent object I began to feel guilty of forgery so I contacted the school again to request my own and to my surprise they responded favourably and even proposed to hire me to design them for the whole course. I had already designed my card to my liking so this turn of event proved that one should never take a 'no' for granted. All was going according to serendipity when, before getting the cards to print, I was fired from my job there for an unrelated event. Some people would call this instant karma.

A business card-sized
miniature postcard depicting Globen, Stockholm

Globen is an indoor arena in Stockholm that was built in 1989. It's hosted the Dalai Lama, Lady Gaga, Eminem, and Miley Cyrus over the years, alongside the most important hockey games in Scandinavia. For a modest sum, one can take a lift on the outside of the spherical building. It's rather unspectacular on top but when I got there I did wonder what it was exactly I had been expecting. The building is the largest spherical man-made object in the world, recalling a golf ball. One day a friend of mine turned to me and simply said: 'Imagine the size of the golf club you'd need to hit that ball', before literally falling off his stool laughing.

As someone who'd only played crazy golf, the joke had little effect on me, despite understanding the scale-related contextual displacement. It wasn't cynicism or my lack of knowledge of a specific sport that left me cold. I do appreciate the size of the golf club it would take to hit that ball, but Globen was otherwise a much bigger object altogether. If you went to the Museum of Natural History in Stockholm it would be very easy to overlook a small spherical object attached to a pillar in front of the front desk in the main hall. Eighteen centimetres wide, this inconspicuous sphere is a model of the moon. Twenty centimetres away is a model of the Earth.

In the mid-nineties, Nils Brenning, at the Royal Institute of Technology in Stockholm, and Gösta Gahm, at the Stockholm University, started the Sweden Solar System project based on the observation that Globen could be considered the model for the Sun scaled down 20,000,000 times. Since then all the planets of the solar system have been placed accordingly throughout the city and beyond, such as the dwarf planet Pluto at 300km from the globe. It is effectively the biggest solar system model on earth. The furthest object is almost 1000km away: the termination shock.

This beautiful project finds its natural limitation because of the curvature of the other object it sits on, Earth itself. Essentially there are near stars that are further away than the circumference of the earth. As the comedian Steven Wright said: 'Everywhere is within walking distance if you have the time.'

A sepia-tone photograph
featuring six young men posing in front of the sea

In 2013, some of my colleagues and I were invited
to Genova as guest tutors for the second part of a
month-long workshop. Giorgio Andreotta Calò had
led the first two weeks, during which time he and the
15 participants had walked silently along the coast of
Italy. On the last day of this extremely testing trip we
met the participants to take over the lead. It was then
we realised the difficulty of the situation. Have you
ever joined a class after it has already started? The
bonds were already built. Everyone was welcoming
but we understood why Giorgio had strongly insisted
on 'going first'.

Over the next two weeks we slowly got to know
each other, while the shadow of the overpowering
previous project was cast on many activities and discussions we could have on and off 'working hours'.
I personally love round the clock workshops, even
if sometimes they can feel like a glorified Big Brother
reality television show. Things do happen without
interruption and it is near impossible to define what
is not work or, more possibly stressful, what is. Discussions would invariably veer from formal attributes
of a sculpture or a book read, to the more personal
problems of a couple formed and dissolved within
the temporary autonomous zone of the workshop.

On one such evening I decided to show the content of my wallet to Lisa, Antoine and Hans. The first object I took out was a passport photo of Andy Warhol wearing his wig and sunglasses. The photo came from a flyer of an exhibition but since one of the photos was an actual passport-size portrait I had cut it out to be able to tell a story of how he could be at several places at once as people would be dazzled by the wig, sunglasses and characteristic camp voice, all of which could rather be easily imitated. Lisa then took out a photo which could have been from the 1950s portraying six young men by the beach, in front of what could be public changing cabins on stilts. One of them appeared to wear a swimsuit.

Lisa said she had found this photo on this very beach while on this long walk. She'd picked it up but had forgotten about it. We all looked at it like a piece of history belonging to strangers but then Lisa, on looking closer, became agitated and livid despite the bronze halo of her face acquired from weeks of outdoor activities in Italy during the Summer. 'What is it?' we asked. Lisa began trembling but managed to say that one of the men, the third one along, was her grandfather. It seemed impossible. Lisa is Dutch and so is her grandfather. To her knowledge he never came to Italy although he is a quarter Albanian from his mother's side. We gasped at the resemblance and

tried to calculate the years, speculate on the possibilities. When Gudrun joined the agitated discussion
she looked and exclaimed that she had seen this very
man during the walk when they went swimming on
the last day.

The Knife is a name I gave my wallet, much in the same way people name a boat, a pet or a villa. Would you name your boat 'Titanic', your cat 'fish' or your chalet in the Alps the address of your primary house in the suburbs of Paris? The answer for at least two of these is 'yes'. An old saying in French mentions one should always carry a knife as one of two essential items.

Whenever finding a dry corner in a pub and a willing spectator, whether I knew them or not, depending on my degree of intoxication, I would propose a guided tour of the contents of my wallet. Sometimes the more enthusiastic member(s) of the audience would offer an object, or at least share a story they found relevant, to be added to the wallet-collection. Imagine if people did this at the end of visiting the Louvre or Tate Modern, bringing back their own painting or installation as a gesture of conviviality (magnanimously partaking in the construction of art heritage).

It so happens that the modesty of the wallet and the casual anecdotes of the tour often sees the visitor take their own wallet out and offer something from it. In Toronto a young artist gave me a card with a big smile. He and the four other audience of the wallet tour had been smiling along, showing interests in the warmest way making the tour one of the longest. I had spoken for nearly two hours.

A short silence closed the end of the tour before David took a card from his own wallet. A single sentence was printed on one side, nothing on the other: 'Went to America, didn't say a word'. He looked at me with intense blue eyes. I could feel the other people's smiles. Would I break this moment by asking what it meant? Do I know what it means? My assumption was that an artist made this but was it relevant? David never said anything and I never asked.

The card reminded me of going to Los Angeles for the first time, without a car, a defying European willing to prove to locals that public transport was key and fully functioning. I tried to reach downtown hopping on random buses and to see the Hollywood sign, a right to the tourist I was although I was there for work close to LAX. I walked for hours and rode bumpy buses never used by either tourists or Europeans, making me suspicious as to how the transport system was designed to bus specific people to specific locations of labour. Why was the bus zigzagging so much if not to deploy the cohorts of cleaners of villas and their pools? On the fourth day I gave up on seeing the giant sign I'd seen many times in my mind anyway: 'Went to LA, didn't see Hollywood'.

A business card for Piet Mondrian

While searching for cheap means of printing I stumbled across the Vistaprint© online printing platform and their unbeatable deal of 150 business cards printed for free in return for their website address on the back. Your own business card would become an advert for their services every time you met a new person. If I wear a Nike t-shirt I pay to become a human-size advert but at the very least I could subscribe to it because I do want to belong to the tribe of whoever thinks Nike is cool. I'm really not sure whether anyone would wear a Vistaprint© suit just because it was free. 'Nothing is more expensive than free stuff,' my mother would say.

An additional attribute of the offer is that one can customise the design based on hundreds of templates available. Not many people would be able to afford the consultancy of a graphic designer who would then work with a producer, namely a printer who wouldn't make less than 2000 cards, the very minimum to set an offset printing press. Even if they were to make 150 it would cost just the same and they'd throw the rest away. Digital printing means one can print-on-demand and minimum quantities are reduced considerably. The services of a graphic designer still seem to be necessary for most professional companies and institutions but Vistaprint© would target the myriad of new professionals, self-employed armies of small businesses in the third sector: yoga teachers, flower shops or ironic graphic designers.

The templates are cliché designs of colours, shapes and other formal attributes that, like photo stock, can reflect some individuality when combined with different typefaces. If there are hundreds of templates, it is also because of the colour combinations and essentially the choice is rather dull. To be fair, let's say whoever designed them is not proud of it.

There was one design that appealed to me: a faux Mondrian-like pattern that could suggest a taste for modern art, appreciation of abstraction and the embrace of less is more. Needless to say, just like L'Oréal or other companies diluting the work of Mondrian to sell their products, it is done without the consent of the family or foundation. The bastardisation is extreme. So much so that I was happily shocked to see the use of green in the pattern offered by Vistaprint©. Green is a colour so hated and dismissed by the modern painter that to see this today would probably make him wake from his grave to come and rant on social media about it. I then decided to make a business card for him at the very address he is today, the cypress hill cemetery in New York.

Flight 93 National Memorial direction card

I found this photocopied card on a display stand at the ticket entrance to Fallingwater, also known as the Kaufman residence. Most people with the faintest interest in architecture would recognise the iconic image of this house in the woods sitting in unison with a waterfall which runs through it, united as the perfect example of what rich people with taste can really afford to build when they cross path with visionaries like Frank Lloyd Wright.

I was close enough to take a photo of the house but I didn't visit the landmark because it was forbidden to children, even those strapped to a Babybjörn. I imagined the strong horizontals and verticals, the place of entertainment of the elite from the 1940s and 1950s ooohing and aaahhhing at the magnificent views from the wide balconies while the inside is cosy and reassuringly protected from the nature one can see in all direction.

I always browse at the leaflets, full-colour A4 on coated paper with glossy images, of the museums, landmarks and other tourist attractions but this time I was attracted to a small display stand in which there were modest photocopied pieces of paper, some pink, some blue, but mainly white 80gsm, with text only. I could imagine them being made in an office on extra time by an enthusiastic fan of Pennsylvania.

None of them had images but were very simple instructions of how to get to another landmark more or less from Fallingwater.

It reminded me of a billboard in London by the artist Adam Chodzko with instructions to how to get somewhere in the States where another billboard would be awaiting with instructions to get to the London one. Reading the instructions it feels difficult to follow especially when one has access to GPS. On my trip across America I failed to refuse the GPS but quickly decided I would only use it for emergencies because it became obvious that this voice, either male or female, was very helpful in getting somewhere but lacked the understanding of the poetry of letting oneself turn left because of an animal instinct or the opposite, trying something against one's better judgement.

I liked the effort of proposing an analog version of 'if you liked this, try that' and picked up a few of them. The only one I have left is of Flight 93 National Memorial because I thought of how open-minded the person making those notes would be to propose the visit of a memorial for a plane which crashed when its passengers took over the terrorists who were going to use it as a weapon to crash into the Capitol Building. When I picked up this card, Al-Qaeda leader Osama Bin Laden was still alive and the terrorist threat a reality.

There are many ways to visit a city: I favour the local fish market, the natural history museum, the neighbourhood of the embassies, a supermarket and a metro, in that particular order. I'll try to avoid making judgemental comparisons about how Mancunian fruits and vegetables are less good looking and tasty than their counterparts in Rennes or Naples. A trip to the metro offers a fast-track entry into the reality of any city. The smell of Châtelet-Les-Halles in Paris is a reminder that at that depth you need as much machinery to allow users to even breathe. The wooden steps of long escalators in London — the first in the world and therefore less efficient than more recent ones like in Singapore — tells us how old they are and of empires, crumbling and emerging.

I was excited to enter the Caracas metro in the USA-defying country that was Venezuela in 2008, a fossil fuel economic power with an intriguing leader at its helm. Petrol there was cheaper than bottled water and, despite everyone seemingly owning a car, the metro system was busy and impeccably clean. Perhaps the state of public transport is a good indication of the health of a country or at least its intentions towards its citizens? It was with some surprise that I held the metro ticket I had just bought. A very familiar paper object for anyone who grew up in

1980s Paris, the ticket is yellow with a brown stripe in a different texture because the ink is mixed with magnetic particles. I was puzzled by the westward geographical jump to South America being accompanied by a backflip in time.

I pictured the diplomatic travels during which elected officials were meeting their counterparts in other countries, industrialists in their trail for deals such as constructing the metro. I imagined the French company making the tickets reassuring the Venezuelan government that the production can only be assured in France and that every ticket would have to be imported, travelling half the world before its single use and being discarded. I can see how they could save on design fees for reusing an obsolete design in the so-called first world or perhaps it was the same design in a fraternal nod to linking Paris and Caracas by their underground passport. Of the twins, only one would still favour the good old design while the other went on to more debatable trendy clothes because of peer pressure.

Ten years on from then the political situation in Venezuela has deteriorated. Chavez is dead and the country is in crisis. How do we know this? The Caracas metro company cannot afford to buy the tickets anymore and subsequently have unblocked the gates so people ride the metro for free.

be trouble if people actually did make those houses (who would be responsible if it collapsed?). It could happen in a world where lawyers would always win arguments as to do less in order to not risk more, such as avoiding the invention of the plane as an aim to avoid inventing the plane crash.

A soiled white plastic card
with rounded edges the size of a Visa card.
A sentence is printed in the middle on one side:
'I EAT LUNCH BETWEEN TWO HIGHWAYS'.

Easily the most prevalent mode of communication is the contractually tacit small talk, understood in opposition, one would think, to big talk, even if it's never defined as such. My seven-year-old daughter, an otherwise polite and relatively patient child, often remarks that adults are chatterboxes. She herself enjoys discussing matters, asking questions, jousting, even, as she discovers the joys and pitfalls of humour and irony. She doesn't enjoy participating in, or even hearing, the constant unresolved treadmill of casual conversation which, let's be honest, leaves many of us in a paradoxical state of vacancy while, for once, interacting with a human being as opposed to passive consumption of data from a smartphone (it is the phone that is smart).

In BS Johnson's 1969 film *Paradigm*, a naked young man enthusiastically utters words and sentences that only make sense to him. In subsequent scenes he ages and wears more and more clothes while saying less and less, growing more tired and expressionless.

The Knife is the name I gave my wallet. Or, more accurately, the guided tour of its contents, which gets extended to the neighbouring phone, pocket detritus or occasional occupants. As I lay the content of the wallet slowly on a table or any surface of a public space I sometimes discard some elements based on an illogical reading of a stranger's face: she won't like this or he won't be interested in that. The way I describe the object also depends on the reactions and conversations with the visitor(s). I have, on occasion, shortened the visit because a conversation prompted by one of the exhibits seemed more interesting than to continue the linked presentation.

As with most guides, I would be the one speaking the most but inevitably — and this is the conversational nature of The Knife — the visitor would pick something out of their wallet and describe the circumstances of their presence there. They would often gift me the object and its story for my collection. Although I would accept all gifts, it'd never come with any guarantees they would be talked about in the next presentation of the display. This card was given to me by a complete stranger on a visit to Poland. He put the card in the middle of the other items and never spoke a word while we all looked at him, waiting for a verbal caption.

Yaïr Barelli's business card

One day, when we already knew each other quite well, Yaïr Barelli gave me his card. I wasn't surprised — it's the sort of thing he does: seemingly pointless but wait, there must be something else to it. The card is poorly designed, even by my standards. The typeface is bland, the paper commonly cheap and the layout carefully set by default. The usual quality or charm of the child's innocence or outsider's fantasy are absolutely absent. The card is truly awful and therefore with many qualities.

The information is layered on a photo of a brownish carpet wallpaper. One can see the lower part of a man. He wears a white t-shirt, a pair of blue jeans and white trainers — the typical effortless white male. By effortless I mean the man who makes no effort because he is predominant and lazy. He is reclining against the wall and even though we cannot see his upper body or face we sense the satisfaction of a job well done in the way he is crossing his feet. He has a gun, of course, a power drill, and a gadget belt with tools no real worker would ever have.

It is rather obvious he is not a professional but a hobbyist who can just about manage to build a shelf on consecutive Sundays over a period long enough for a woman to become pregnant and give birth. The photo is a typical stock image, a cliché for hire that can be used dialectically to say something and its opposite. It is fit for advertisement as well as ironic memes.

Yaïr is a man in his thirties. He is tanned, handsome, smart and funny. Very charming and systematically questioning, he was satisfied when I once called him an artist who works with dance rather than a dancer who is an artist. He makes money being a dancer for successful choreographers while his aspirations and practice leads him naturally outside of the theatre where most dance operations take place. He is one of the rare people bridging contemporary art and dance.

I look at the card and think that perhaps Yaïr is suggesting he can fix things in ways unexpected, that while I can think of him as a dancer he can actually make a shelf during the time a woman can get pregnant and give birth. Perhaps it is metaphorical and shows intent to want to solve questions by using other means than what he was educated for. It also shows a sense of irony and humour. I also think he is playing with me, a highly educated graphic designer whose work he finds unqualified and poor.

We give workshops together and one of his favourite pastimes is to show the students examples of my graphic design work without telling them who authored them in order to see them criticise it harshly, which is one hundred per cent of the time.

This card is made on the Vistaprint© platform and therefore tells me Yaïr's financial situation makes him compromise with poor quality service because it is free (on the back of the card is the web address of the printing company). He would not, however go with a design that would be a typical image of an artist — brush strokes of many colours, drippings or a hand with clay. Today the service has upped its standards with digital technology advancement and finishing touches such as foiling, coloured-edges or embossing. The website even proposes a ten-point advice page on design that is commonsense but certainly useful such as making sure it represents you, that one should proofread or employ the back for additional use (calendar?) and they conclude with the tenth point. If in doubt talk to a designer.

'Sorry' card

I found this card in a box full of printed matter related to exhibitions: programs, flyers, posters and invitations. It has a single word on it, in Times New Roman, in black and raised so one can feel the letters by touch: 'Sorry'. The paper is elegant and mildly heavy, harder than the standard flimsy calling cards. I have no recollection of being given it but I can assume it was in an art context, possibly it was an unlimited edition. There is no other information on it, such as a signature or even worse a website address. I tried to Google 'business card sorry' and nothing came up so I cannot credit the artist who made this.

Wales-based artist Bedwyr Williams once told me a story about seeing a beach towel drying on a balcony in Venice when he lived there for a residency. The towel had a picture of the World Trade Center printed on it in vivid colours. At first he was amazed by it and the perfectly strange combination of timing and location. A torrent of questions struck him at the same time: Who did this belong to? How did it get here? Could this feeling be the encounter with art as a concept? Almost immediately, and as forceful as the initial emotion, a thought came to destroy everything: this towel was an artist's work.

€0 banknote

Nothing is ever free and that includes this €0 banknote. I bought it for €2 from a vending machine just outside the Oceanographic Museum in Monaco for the pleasure of experiencing a paradox: inserting two metal coins to get a piece of paper that stated it had no monetary value. Of course, this is a currency because as long as people continue buying them people will continue producing them. I enjoyed this encounter, occurring at the end of a warm day, after a fruitful meeting, in the unique place that is Monaco. This banknote isn't really a fake as it is authorised by the Central European Bank and produced in the same way banknotes are, using the same paper and printing security features. In a way, this is a robbery of the bank with the bank itself as an accomplice. It is telling that the bank would produce souvenir banknotes to make more money.

After I'd had the experience of buying money with money and losing 100% of the value in doing so I wondered what to do with it except adding it to The Knife. My first reaction was to relish the idea of discussing this object with my daughter who would have questions I couldn't possibly answer. The same evening I went to a student party in a different city and realised that I had no cash on me at the bar. They wouldn't take plastic so I just took out the €0 note in the hope that something might happen. The bartender, a young student in her first year at this art college, looked at it and laughed. She was so happy that she put the note in her own pocket and told me I could have drinks all night with this, which I did and woke the next day with a terrible hangover.

'NO FORMULA ONE NO CRY' taxi card

This card was found among flyers in an art Institution in the early 2000s. I'm not sure where but it was clearly the work of an artist — a work that is of something we are familiar with but also something else. On the back is four or five names followed by a city and a mobile number. It seems personal to have the name of a taxi driver and the list of cities. It seems random and yet clearly indicates that this is someone's list that is being shared with us.

I always carried this card with me, intrigued by what it suggested. I never Googled it although someone I showed it to said it was the work of French Albanian artist Anri Sala. He and I went to the same school in Paris. He was one of the only two non-French students at the L'École nationale supérieure des Arts Décoratifs and arrived in the third year. He was already working on a beautiful film about the youth of his mother as a political activist. There was a determination in his attitude that was admirable as most of us were having the protected fun an art school can provide, creating the shock of what happens next.

Fifteen years later Anri would represent France at the Venice Biennial. The knowledge of the author didn't give me a clue about the nature of this work — the films of his that I knew wouldn't point at this kind of art embedded in the social interaction with a taxi driver. I have been to all the cities on the card twice now but never dared calling. How long does one keep the same number or the same job these days?

A Caffé Nero loyalty card

This loyalty card promises the bearer a free coffee after the ninth purchase. You could be a group of ten and immediately get your free coffee or go there everyday and get the card stamped nine times before exchanging it for the anticipated beverage. This specific card has the tenth coffee torn. I am a coffee drinker but am unable to follow the fidelity or loyalty scheme of corporate chains because of a work pattern that doesn't follow any oder, mixed with a sudden change of mind in drinking tea or hot water for a while, not to mention the puerile aversion to being the client of mega corporations when it comes to the dark drink despite having to admit defeat that yes coffee was awful in the States before Starbucks.

This card is more of a reminder of *Remainder*, the first novel by Tom McCarthy, whose hero buys coffee towards the end of the story in an airport. After purchasing nine he only drinks the tenth freebie. This loyalty card is my physical ticket to the fictitious world of the novel, even if I must confess that while the mysterious action made perfect sense as the apotheosis of the book, I am unable to remember why this prompted me to create a real object from a fictional world, which is only fair considering that the main character has a memory problem and, like most of us, goes on a quest to find himself.

As a comic-book reading teenager and a fan of Alan Moore's *The Watchmen* I had replicated a photograph from the story as an actual-sized artefact I could hold. It was difficult then to rationalise it, only the drive was strong enough to continue. As an adult I am none the wiser except I can just call it work.

Chevron Corporation is an American multinational energy company. As a provider of fossil fuels, also known as gas there, petrol here, its logo can be seen pretty much everywhere in the United States. It is very true the American roads can become rather wild and the vastness of its nature can come as a surprise to Europeans. Commercial signage is often the only indication that humans do exist within a humbling demonstration of force by nature that only does what it does: exist. We are very small indeed and the metal shelter of a moving car psychologically provides a small consolation to the inevitable existential questions one is faced with, wondering whether ants do feel the same way on the edge of the Grand Canyon.

In any road trips in these magnificent deserted areas the familiar light box of a petrol station can become as heart-warming as the conversation with a dear friend. You are at night, having driven ten hours, singing less and less heartily as you cannot help no-ticing the little gas pump light going on, indicating the vehicle's thirst. It was in one of those moments and places that this very card was picked up on Lone Pine Chevron station in California after a long ride without seeing any other cars in a torrential rain that created doubts in our minds (does the rain fall harder when no humans are around?). Looking at the station and the associated business card/flyer, it could be striking that for a corporation this big, they seem to trust their franchised stations to handle the design identity with a strong personal touch. Lee, the boss and only employee, did look very much like its cartoon representation, drawn by Kraske who managed to sign his work on a business card.

Lee: 'Hi Kraske, I need a flyer for my petrol station, the business is a little slow.'

Kraske: 'Okay, no problem but I told you I am not a corporate designer so I'm not sure if you'd want to hire me. Then again, I could do with the cash.'

L: 'Yes, don't worry I will not even show it to my bosses, you know they hardly know I exist, being isolated here and Samuel who brings the gas is the only guy I ever see from them. When I went to that Chevron employees meeting in Aspen they did say as long as the logo is blue and red, it's all fine. I'm pretty sure it wasn't a joke. Remember that for the lightbox sign I kept the old one three years because they had forgotten me.'

K: 'Okay, cool that's the way I see it. I'm gonna draw you holding that gas pistol and in the other hand Mount Whitney cos it's beautiful and I know you like climbing it, making it personal. People should know it's your place so we'll have 'Lee's frontier liquor' in big type, also because, let's face it, we all buy our alcohol at yours more than get gas.'

L: 'Yeah, and don't forget to mention the free coffee, the fishing bait I specially make myself with my secret ingredients, the sports stuff, the wine, the beer...'

K: 'And the guns.'

L: 'AND ICE! In the desert, that's gold.'

K: 'You want to make business? Then let's not make a flyer but a business card so people can keep it in their wallets. It's a lot of info but I'm sure it fits.'

L: 'Awesome.'

K: 'I have an idea about the logo, it can be on the top of the card but the drawing will go ON it, that's how I feel about The Man.'

L: 'Yeah but The Man is paying you so show some respect.'

K: 'Mm, fine, how about I draw you wearing the Chevron patch on your sleeve, so you'd be saying you respect them?'

L: 'Deal. We keep both ideas.'

Lee and Kraske are the same person. We've all done it before, we all speak to our other self. Don't you?

When thinking of fly posted advertisements, the pre-internet way, it might be wise to consider the distribution network of such a flyer. Lee's station is isolated but for whoever drives to Lone Pine almost impossible to miss. The advertisement, if not the self-imposing billboard, needs the human apparatus of architectural context. You can't just leave your flyers on the ground, they just are considered trash and nature will make sure it is taken care of without having reached your potential customers.

Lee thought about this and he started giving his cards to truck drivers and occasional tourists. More than one card, so they themselves distribute the ads. He also started giving them away to the sparse ~~houses~~ around, just in case. They knew each other so the purpose of the advert was void but a courtesy visit and a tea or beer that went with it was always welcomed. He was always proud to hand them to the customers although they would most likely never pass by the place again. Of course Lee is as friendly as his card so the human interaction prompted by a piece of printed card is tremendous compared to the theoretically sole purpose of the commercial exchange occurring between people in this situation. Some who did not partake in the fishing sport would buy some bait as presents or others would go on Mount Whitney instead of heading back to Los Angeles.

Lee Kraske would appear as the typical smiling American guy, a lovely dude who's always happy to help. It would be difficult to know he is a sixteenth Japanese, although he neither speaks the language nor has ever set foot in Japan. It was a painful irony for him to move there some thirty years ago from San Diego, so close to the Manzanar site of the Japanese concentration camp. As a young enthusiast of Chevron franchise, he made it his duty to know more about the immediate surroundings of his gas station, both the nature and any human-made compounds or buildings and he took himself and his pick up to all the roads within 57 miles, including the clearly indicated dead end roads, which doesn't mean they won't lead you somewhere interesting.

In one such trip he came across the Manzanar historical site, a wooden structure in an otherwise flat desert environment surrounded by the distant mountains. A mere two hours later the jovial Lee was in tears, standing in front of nothing but the remains of a foundation for another similar barrack he saw from the road when he parked. This ghost building was one of the dozens which used to stand there complete in the dusty wind some 65 years earlier. All buildings occupied by Japanese people, American citizens and some, like him, just a sixteenth of a thin-blooded Asian. Like him, some prisoners did not remotely look oriental. It is perhaps little known

126

that more than 100,000 people of Japanese descent were interned in this very place after the attack on Pearl Harbour in 1942. The US government had taken drastic measures to avoid a conflict of patriotism some American immigrants could suffer and so the American Concentration Camp of Manzanar was open.

A green card

Betsy Bickle is an American designer and visual identity consultant. She was born in 1950 in Atlanta. When she was in her twenties she campaigned for the local democrats until she went to New York to study communication and advertising design. Bickle has always believed in the role of design in the constitution of society. Paul Rand and other modernists are her role models in terms of thoughts, if not necessarily in forms.

This green business card was part of a package she sent as an unsolicited proposal to colonel Muammar Gaddafi in 1981. Her belief in left-wing politics, the general fear and madness of the cold war, led her into circles of young people who would gather until the early hours of the night, recreating a world more just. In 1976 an English friend of hers came back from London with the green book, the English translation of Gaddafi's political thoughts. Betsy was intrigued and enthralled. As a designer she was also fascinated by the decision of branding the flag as a monochrome green — no other countries had a monochrome flag, the surrendering white flag being a tool for all.

Was the green in opposition or at least an alternative to the communist red and capitalist blue, a third way as proposed by the non-aligned countries attempting to create space between the massive superpowers of the cold war? A little later she would wonder if red and blue were obvious western oppositions — Coca Cola versus Pepsi or the Bloods versus the Crips. Green could be linked to Islam but not all Muslim countries chise green in their identity.

She was, however, excited by the bold move yet did not think it went far enough. She went on to work on a complete visual identity for the Libyan Arab Jamahiriya with two of the interns at the ad agency she worked at as a senior art director. The 240-page proposal ranged from logos, visual identity rules, uniforms and tools, motorway signs, vehicles, buildings and even food, the latter including working closely with agro-engineers to develop a food staple more green than mother nature alone would have planned.

Green inks would be used for all written messages instead of the more conventional black. Bickle suggested the change for offset print process from a four colour cyan magenta, yellow and black to, according to her, a more economical three colour magenta, green and black. The green card, a mock up of what should inherently be made from green paper pulp rather than white card printed came with the following explanation:

'If you decide that green becomes your colour, then this is how they will know you, the only people confident enough to go all the way. This business card is a modest introduction to your radical ideas. It denies them the usual information but focuses on the more important concept of your political views, your Third Way. If they need to know your name or of anyone in the government, they must make the effort. I also suggest this card to be common to all governmental bodies and people. You will have the same business card as your ambassador in Cuba or the local policeman.'

BUSINESS card

A piece of white card with the word 'BUSINESS' printed on one side. An American artist gave me this card at the end of a guided tour of the wallet, this time in a classroom, a beamer showing on the wall the items on the desk. His smile expressed the confidence of having found a like-minded person who would understand the implication of a tautological business card that announced itself as a BUSINESS-making device while withholding any of the usual useful information for the purpose of making business. No way to communicate via telephone or social media, even send packages to a terrestrial address, or to even know who we are doing business with by being able to call the other person by last name first and, who knows, after a while by the first name. As I am writing this, the lack of printed information eludes my wish to credit the artist who was in his mid twenties, male, white, short dark hair, handsome and smiling, living in Chicago at the time. If you read this and need to manifest yourself please contact the publishing house.

A job title is equally useful when the business is bigger than a sole trader. When tautology is at work there is a fine line between conceptual art and the practical joke. A cat is called 'Cat' or a business card bears the word 'BUSINESS'. The latter might be found in those once-popular joke shops and get a smile from the browsing customer but it is likely the quick fix won't last enough for the purchase to happen. On the other hand, one could imagine that if president John Fitzgerald Kennedy had presented this card to USSR general secretary Nikita Krushchev during their only meeting at the height of the cold war, very very close to human annihilation, the performative art would have been one of legend. Keeping a straight face, disconcertingly taking jokes towards unknown territories to unlock small talks. Way to go.

Charlotte York's business card

Laminated double-sided business card, an image on one side, the details of a Charlotte York on the other, working for Sean Kelly gallery in New York. On closer inspection, the caption for an artwork by *Marina Abramovic* is printed in gloss varnish, visible only when the gloss catches light from handling the card at a certain angle.

In an episode of the nineties TV series *Sex and the City* one of the main characters is shown in a contemporary art gallery witnessing a durational performance by a female artist in her pyjamas, supposedly spending 24 hours a day, for days on end, in room-sized cubes affixed to the wall. The room seems to be accessible by a ladder but the steps are made of large kitchen knives, signifying, without the subtlety of any doubt, that the artist is trapped up there, in front of visitors during gallery hours and on her own when the place is closed.

Carrie Bradshaw murmurs to her friend that she cannot believe in the self-inflicted ordeal and that the artist probably goes home every evening to her luxury loft and eats at will. Her friend condemns the artist's hair style, sending both of them into cheeky suppressed laughter that we understand as a message to the other visitors of the gallery's meaning: Do you know how stiff you guys are while we are cool about it? Come on, why so serious? A good-looking man in his fifties hears Carrie and turns around to discover this philistine is a pretty middle-aged woman. Carrie, being an intelligent art loving New York cool cat, appears to feel shame and flusters at yet another sexy man taking interest in her, albeit who scorn her for disrespectful behaviour in the sanctified space of the white cube.

The man approaches in the suavest crab-inspired body shift and invites Carrie to a candlelit dinner, to which she obliges. During the romantic *tête-à-tête* the man reveals himself to also be an artist and in a gesture of solidarity towards his fellow performance artist brings Carrie back to the gallery to make a point — his importance asserted by the fact he has round-the-clock access to the gallery. Once there he is satisfied to impress his date by proving that the conceptual performer is as radical as the press release states and is still performing in the absence of a public.

The woman in question is an actress but the work itself is real and so is the gallery one can see in the episode. The installation and the performative act is an artwork called *The house with the Ocean View* (2002) by Marina Abramović. The Serbian artist declined to play her own role but agreed for the work to appear in this mainstream TV series which she had never heard of. It is debatable how or why the actress was to wear an ugly wig, possibly to allow the main characters who are usually obsessed with their appearance to comment on her for the story to develop.

He wears black skinny jeans. His back pocket is marked by a circle, a crop mark made by a plastic box of snus that lived there for years. In his native Sweden the wet tobacco pouches sold in round plastic containers are the companions of any cool kid and the used circle on jeans pockets would certify this attitude to whoever glances at your buttocks on the street. Some of his classmates forcefully grinded the box and the jeans against the giant stones scattered around Stockholm. Not him.

Two decades later the jeans still fit, the hair is still long, however peppered it is by natural time travelling. The nicotine habits have passed away but the pocket is today full of 666 euros worth of shredded money. His right hand almost permanently lives in the pocket, deep in the decadent dry bath.

He awaits for the celebratory confetti moment. Any time now, anytime…

Kiss my queen

She appeared on a white Vespa, with a golden helmet, a perfect sunrise crowning her when she gracefully took it off. Her hand slid down inside the breast pocket of her leather jacket. You see the heptagon coin between her fingers. She shows you the familiar profile of Elizabeth II. She solemnly kisses the queen, the sun disappearing between their lips. She flicks it in the air and you truly see it spinning in slow motion. As it lands she shows you the queen's been transformed into a well-dressed frog.

Flattened oval souvenir coin
(from Mount Rushmore, USA,
Musée de la Mer, Cherbourg,
Science Museum, London,
Stedelijk Museum, Amsterdam)

For the modest sum of £1.01, €1.01 or $1.01 a mechanical device strategically placed next to a landmark or museum transforms part of your means of payment into a site-specific souvenir. The machine, mechanically operated by the customer, is in a see-through box, showing the cogs and crannies that take the smaller coin through a male/female engraving device resulting in an oval-shaped medal.

The more civic-minded of us will wonder how one could impudently deface government property, while the magic enthusiast will appreciate that a single president (Abraham Lincoln) adorning a one-cent coin can, for instance, be transformed into four (George Washington, Thomas Jefferson, Theodore Roosevelt and… Abraham Lincoln) at the Mount Rushmore souvenir shop. The eagle-eyed will still see the ghostly presence of an elongated Lincoln in the background of the rocky mountain ridge.

A coin with a central hole,
both sides marked
'AGE COIN'

All Japanese coins once had holes so that a string would replace the purse (inside vs outside?) and were kept in the oversized sleeves of an otherwise pocketless kimono. Move forward at least a century to the Netherlands and you will find this particular design for a coin. It cannot buy you anything but the right to use a cigarette vending machine. They can be found in a plastic cup at the bar, more or less under the vigilance of the bartenders, who are able to distinguish the adults from the children, who are neither allowed to drink or smoke.

The age of a coin is most visible on British currency where Elizabeth II, the longest-serving queen, grace-fully ages in a more realistic manner on the coins, including a royal double chin and wisdom wrinkles. May she reign for over one hundred years so we can see her profile then. Probably she will survive paper and metal money, appearing, even, on digital currencies where she could age in real time.

A dollar bill blind embossed with the sentence
'A group of people standing outside of a closed
day centre'

This dollar bill was blind embossed by a visitor to Jeremy Deller's exhibition 'Joy in People' at WIELS Contemporary Art Centre in Brussels, 2012. In this retrospective of the British artist it was possible to interact with blind embossing machines and perhaps bring back a piece of art as much as one's belief in the infra-thin power of it. One immediate consequence to such an installation is the realisation of the material self or being aware of what one carries, one wears. Some people will emboss a banknote, others a bus ticket, most the press release of the show. Occasionally one visitor will try to emboss her shirt or his finger but generally an almost exhaustive list of possibilities can be drawn.

Almost ten years prior, the Mexican artist Minerva Cuevas presented an installation at Musée d'Art moderne de la Ville de Paris in which one encountered a big table with what seemed a lot of rubbish on it. A well-meaning invigilator would explain that the artist had brought something on this offering table to be exchanged by visitors. It was obvious that most obliged and were confronted by the poor content of their pockets or bags because of where they were: visiting a museum on a Sunday. It is highly possible a gregarious attitude authorised many to discharge what is essentially trash such as used tickets, unwanted flyers, half empty water bottles, paper tissues, although none soiled, illustrating the complexity — or is it simplicity? — of bartering when the double coincidental and in the end exceptional occasion of encountering a person who possesses something one wants and beautifully wishes to relinquish it for the exact thing one is willing to give away? Try this while abstaining from creating debt.

Arthur Lloyd's business card

This business card is inscribed with 'Human card index' and, below: 'Any printed items on request'. Arthur Lloyd was an American entertainer whose hardly-documented practice was based on having memorised the alleged 5000 printed items he would carry in his academic robe. A member of the audience would say anything and Arthur would pull out from within his robe a printed item to match what was said.

Artist Aurélien Froment became interested in the techniques of memory Lloyd had developed and adapted from previous researchers, as well as the devices employed, specifically a robe able to physically carry 5000 cards, tickets, certificates, letters, and stamps. It is one thing to hear a story, yet another to verify how apocryphal it is. Five thousand items of printed matter at 5g each amounts to 25kg.

A robe would need to be made of fabric that could support the weight as much as the pockets to distribute the cards more or less evenly. The aim here is not to debunk what we probably all missed, not having lived in the early twentieth century when Lloyd was performing his act. The fascinating question to a generation living in parallel to the seemingly infinite cloud-busting internet storage space is this: could the world — be it limited to the Western one — be contained within only 5000 items of printed matter?

birth certificate,
love letter,
college diploma,
pre-nuptial settlement,
autopsy report.
The End.

The challenging moments are whenever cultural difference allows for mistranslation of stories. It might be a lack of self-confidence at speaking at length but sometimes drug-induced stories and sexual content are not appropriate for a devout believer or seven-year-old. I like to think that it's an editorial decision, or even a personal ethical decision, as to what is being talked about and when. Both the necro card by Stuart Home and the donor card by Carey Young are artworks, or at least art editions, that take the NHS donor card as a starting point. Without this for reference it is possibly puzzling to decipher what exactly it is we are looking at (both works are philosophical enquiries into the oft' forgotten mortality of our physical selves).

NHS is the acronym of the National Health Service (it should probably be NHSUK in order to distinguish it from the National Health Service of any other nation than the United Kingdom but a past as a western superpower excludes the United Kingdom the need to over-present itself; The National Health Service is de facto the one of the United Kingdom).

To contextualise these for those not familiar with a donor card, let's just say the original is a card one signs as a testament of wishing one's organs to be used by anyone in need of them once trespassing into the gates of death — the handling of designated organs going through professionals, such as surgeons, as opposed to anyone who finds your corpse. The card itself is not contractual, even if a signature is required, but one can tick a few boxes to choose which parts will or will not find a new body host and its presence functions as a reminder of being humble, perhaps. Movies have explored what can happen when inheriting someone else's eyes or limbs. Stuart Home and Carey Young may have never met. They are both white English artists and, give or take eight years, from the same generation, still alive at the time of writing this. Eight years can be an eternity for people but let's not forget we are much longer dead than alive and after a while eight years is truly a fleck in the scope of infinity. Both cards deal with what happens after death, although in almost opposite ways.

Carey Young's card, an unlimited edition one could find a few years ago within her exhibitions, is signed by the artist and upon signing it yourself it states the card has become an artwork until one of the two signatories dies. At this point the art status of said card will disappear. Stuart Home's card, in contrast, is a bequest for the signatory's corpse to be used sexually. Both cards, however, are reliant on personal belief and personal faith as neither are lawfully endorsed by the UK government. Both of these cards have often been the starting point of longer discussions which became the focus of the evenings without ever returning to visit any of the other items in the wallet — a perfectly fine way to exit the visit without having to go through the gift shop.

Meet
me
outside

You are in a restaurant, alone in an unknown city. A mere three hours earlier you gave a presentation in front of a room full of enthusiastic people, none of whom you knew, except, and that is a surprise, an old friend you just remembered had mentioned would be moving to that city a few years earlier. So many smiles and expectations you feel you delivered. Everything went not only better than the usual but you even allow yourself to consider it was actually rather good. The elocution, the flow, the balance between the written and the improvised was imperceptible. You even didn't let the internal euphoria go over the top in a cringing joke like you often do, shattering the hardly-built house of cards.

The two people who invited you, one nice stranger and an old friend who had shed 15kg in the last year and a half since you last saw him, were encouraging during the whole hour session and the exciting Q&A afterwards. People were curious and theirs were real questions, not just an observation which segues to their own obsession and showing off. You did listen to the questions and managed to answer them, not digressing into your own obsessions and showing off, leaving the member of the public frustrated their questions were yet another pedestal for someone who was already on stage, blinded by an automatic mission of spreading the word.

Euphoric is the feeling. You even help the organisers stack the chairs after more than ten people queued to chat to you after the final round of applause, thirsty for yet more interesting conversations and remarks you never thought of, prompting notes to your future self to include in your presentation and research. This is elating and by far the best talk you ever gave, doubled by the guilty knowledge some people were turned down because health and safety were already stretching room capacity.

You are very excited about the after drinks, even if you'll have to excuse yourself not too late because you have a workshop tomorrow in the same city in an unknown university because one has to be reasonable and smelling of booze at tutorials is not rock'n roll. You are happy to see your friend and most positively charmed by the curator who mentioned a few books earlier, showing that you share interests and providing a great introduction to a fruitful discussion at dinner.

Your friend, however, announces that he must leave to go back to the capital by train. You notice there may be later trains but he seems tired. He also is a little more serious than you used to know but you have known people for whom slimming fast equated to slimming their sense of humour. He announces he is going to see his boyfriend. You turn towards the curator who actually invited you to give the talk and remark how the bike helmet she is wearing does suit her and indicate you might cycle to get that drink and this is a good sign because it is not just the first whatever-pub around the corner but a chosen one. She, however, thanks you and, eyes rolling, mentions her babysitter and being late and good luck for everything, will you find your way to the hotel and have a nice journey back tomorrow.

You smile and thank her for the invitation, that it was fantastic and start listing all the interesting remarks and questions you never had thought of and only prompted by the combination of everyone's energy into making this evening worthwhile when you realise she genuinely is worried about her infant being left alone by a time conscious babysitter and so you let her go as she didn't hear anything you said of the last five minutes.

On the pavement outside you expect rain to start but it doesn't. A group of people you vaguely recognise from the audience are talking and the idea of joining them flames in your mind but shame prevents you from approaching. You take your phone out and check a website for an average restaurant where you can go and eat.

You are in a restaurant, alone in an unknown city, and halfway through your meal a person passes your table and leaves a card on the table. You turn the card and its reads: 'Meet me outside'.

Ryan Gander double-sided playing cards

A double-sided card game. Seven of diamond on one side, four of clubs on the other. Ideas, ideas. Ryan Gander has many. This British artist covers the walls of his studio with A4 sheets of paper on which are sentences that could potentially become an artwork. Some ideas are so simply clever it's as if you see a lightbulb appear in front of your eyes, like in cartoons. Others are combinations of words you know but which become indecipherable in the combinations chosen by Ryan.

Ryan's studio walls are covered with ideas, ten of which some artists would be intellectually satisfied with. One of the A4 sheet reads, 'a wall covered with landscape sheets of A4, each printed in black using the same typeface an idea for an artwork'. Everything has potential to become an artwork, even the display system itself, the organisational system, the fact of reading them, the fact of not understanding them, the fact someone describes it elsewhere, the fact those words are being thought.

Ryan's ideas range from the depth of the personal, avant-garde of a species that doesn't exist yet, from being alienating to even the most addicted fan to something you swear you'd seen in a joke shop in a Hong Kong bazaar but actually didn't. Something like, say, a pack of cards with no backs, only fronts, for which you'd have to hire clever people to come up with games to play with.

A €2 coin with a side completely sanded down to erase any relief; the other side shows the Neuschwanstein Castle, identifying the coin as a German commemorative coin

Emmanuel, an intellectual who escaped the art institutions of Paris to become the co-director of a home for children in the countryside of the poorer northern part of France, is a lovely person. He has a broad smile and his kindness could be seen, by protective ironic measures, as disingenuous, especially as it is well known that he himself can be a joker of the kind who never reveals when he is joking or not.

Emmanuel has asked Charlotte to make a present for Pierre-Yves who will soon retire. His way of asking is gentle but impossible to discuss. Charlotte is puzzled by being given an order in such a friendly manner. His request is that it must cost less than €2. This point has been repeated five times using five channels: SMS, email, voicemail, WhatsApp, and finally face to face. It is a riddle Charlotte understands won't be explained or commented on, not now nor ever.

Charlotte is quick to conclude she will sandpaper down a €2 coin in literal response to something which is less than €2. The moment comes: she gives the coin to Pierre-Yves who is quizzical. He doesn't know what this means. At least he and Charlotte agree on this. It doesn't seem to be an in joke between the two men Charlotte was hired to be the interface for. Emmanuel takes out a packaged box for Charlotte who discovers a commemorative €2 coin with General Charles de Gaulle on it. She doesn't get it. Emmanuel is still smiling. What is this all about?

Dream on

In October 2002 I was in Tokyo for some work organised by the British Council, who flew me business class in the most comfortable seat I'd experience in my life. For the first time and, to date, the last I shared the bit most people don't when they enter a plane and are invited to go on the left and not the traditional right after the stewardess checks the boarding pass.

To be fair, the smiles and attitudes are similar but the attention is different. In economy you ask for something, while here in business, staff hover discreetly, making sure you don't notice them while they pour champagne as if by telepathic messaging. The space is different too: a whole bed pod to spend your flight lying down, a mini room from which you can order anything you would want, feeling less and less guilty of feeling being entitled, understanding the mechanisms of luxury blinding you into the justification that anything less than that would be intolerable and whoever accepts it would surely be mad enough to actually like and be satisfied with the situation.

The driver of the limo waiting at the airport with my name spelled correctly on a card made me feel self-conscious of the old trainers I was wearing but I was smelling good from the actual shower I had on the plane and blushed slightly when I said to him, 'That's me!' He was very good at hiding his surprise that a bummy man would be the VIP he'd have to drive but probably decided it wasn't worth asking for identification. The road to central Tokyo, even if it never was that much of a hassle either by luxurious train or comfy buses was totally different from the usual and again a fear of becoming accustomed to the main problem of the world prevented me to spread eagle on the vulgar leather seat.

The driver was taking me to the Hyatt hotel and seeing the massive room I had been granted I started to be suspicious of why a governmental organisation such as the British Council would treat me like royalty when it occurred to me that their call was late and I had heard that some designers would cancel their commitment and a quick replacement would have to be found. If this happens at the end of the tax year the organisation would have to spend cash quick to avoid being penalised for not having spent the money in time and receive less the following year. True or false, it remains I would spend a whole week in a district of Tokyo I barely knew in and out of the hotel with a brilliant restaurant bar on the 52nd floor with a lastingly unique view over Tokyo. Again, seeing ant-like people down there while drinking a cocktail is surely part of the plan to justify the existence of the elite to themselves. I certainly felt the power of tipping generously since it was pretty much the only expenses I had sojourning the lives of the rich others.

On the last day, going to my room, I bumped into a person and my papers, as well as her backpack, went flying in the corridor. She was a blonde American woman in her twenties who helped me gather my things then we both presented excuses bowing like the Japanese we are not and parted ways. As I left I noticed a piece of plastic on the carpet and picked it up as I recognised my magnetic card key for my room. As I arrived at my door the key was not functioning and I remembered putting it in my wallet so how did it manage to be on the floor back there when I bumped into this person? I realised I had this young woman's card. The keys were blank cards for discretion, unlabelled. In an act I cannot really explain I kept the card.

Almost exactly a year later I saw the young woman again but in the cinema. She was the main actress in Sofia Coppola's *Lost in Translation* and her hotel key was in my wallet.

London tube map (September 2009)

In 1983, American illusionist David Copperfield made the Statue of Liberty disappear. This happened on TV for millions and was shot in front of a live audience that gasped at Lady Liberty vanishing and, oh my, could the notion of liberty disappear too? Luckily for democracy the Statue of Liberty reappeared a few minutes later.

In the Autumn of 2009, London commuters and tourists alike were picking up London tube maps in order to orient themselves in the oldest subway system in the world. Some were perhaps admiring the classic design of the map. Such seemingly-evident elegant design of colours, lines and circles were actually invented in the UK by a technical draughtsman called Harry Beck in the 1930s. Some would overlook its design because they had the same at home, in Paris, New York, Moscow or Tokyo, unaware that most subway maps derive from a revolutionary idea Mr Beck once had of going for geometrical logic over geographical accuracy. The map is reprinted periodically and for some time its cover has become a regular commission to contemporary artists.

The very specific edition of September 2009 had a cover by Richard Long, well-known for his walks as artworks in the countryside, a far cry from the underground public transport system of London.

The more noticeable change was not so much the cover but the map itself. In order to declutter what had become a complex map, according to Transport for London executives, zones were erased and as if by magic the river disappeared entirely. All this was made without grand announcement but the Londoners were quick to react, including its mayor who demanded the Thames reappear, which it did in the following edition a few months later. Abracadabra.

A black and white ID photograph
of Andy Warhol scribbled over

When I studied for my art foundation in Paris in the early 1990s we were given a weekly task loosely based, we were told, on a Bauhaus method. The teacher was a scary middle-aged man who'd enjoy humiliating the 100 or so students whose work would be hung in the middle of the room while being trashed for over five minutes each, causing many to cry or at the very least develop confidence issues.

We'd all seen him tear a work because it wasn't the right format or because the borders were too narrow. We were all young adults, old enough to keep parents away from intervening — self-respect please — but 16 – 17 year olds are not exactly prepared for the abusive treatment this man would exact in semi-public. The worse was that despite knowing you'd be next, the crucifixion of someone else would provoke laughter as the devil had certainly an acute sense of humour and dare I say with distance permitting that he was spot on most times, possibly explaining the way nobody objected or confronted him directly. In any case he was destroying souls.

This was 25 years ago and as I conjured his name it hit me. This teacher was Mr André Troublé but we would all call him Troublé, obviously meaning 'troubled' but this had never crossed my mind before

Perpetual French stamp

'Will you love him forever?'
'Did they live happily ever after?'

These are questions okay to be asked but too big to be answered without a fade to black in a cinema. 'Will a stamp last forever?' is another question I wondered about the first time I noticed the absence of value on the French first class stamp. I have since seen the same in other countries. This recent French stamp follows a tradition that states: *lettre prioritaire* (priority or first class, the nuance is the difference between France and the UK), La Poste (the official name of the postal office), France (to distinguish from Canada) and '20g', the weight limit this stamp allows its transport for. Others would have a price but the permanent validity stamp is forever. I could keep it and pass it on to generations and in a thousand years they would have to honour their side of the contract: transporting a letter to any address in France. This tiny piece of self-adhesive printed matter is a testimony to the belief in the solidity of the institution and the nation.

Am I to trust them and believe that the Post Office is forever? My Lebanese friends beg to differ. Even further, am I to believe France will have the same borders or even still exist as a nation? A positive person would find strength in this stamp.

The design, however, changes often and each new president never forgets to commission a new face for Marianne, the symbol of France, a woman of reason and liberty, a bare-breasted defender of Freedom at the forefront of the revolutionary uprising painted by Delacroix and later present on banknotes, seen by every French citizen pretty much everyday.

Marianne never actually existed, which allows artists to give her the face they want, from unknown models to Brigitte Bardot. Like Brigitte Bardot she is the same yet can take the profile the ruling state wants to attribute to her: the sexy and intellectual Godard epoch woman, the later animal rights activist or the dubious extreme right sympathiser. Pick your Marianne.

At least Brigitte Bardot was French, said the offended stamp critiques when it was revealed in 2014 that the new drawing was based on Inna Shevchenko, the Ukrainian leader of the FEMEN, a feminist activist group often demonstrating topless against patriarchy. Does a symbol need a passport?

Monika Gorniak was born 20 April 1926 in Torun, Poland and died 28 December 2004 in Cheyenne, Wyoming. She emigrated to the US when she was 11 years old, following her mother on the transatlantic journey from Rotterdam. Monika always showed a strong individualism and her constant need for freedom led her to live the life of the American hobo after her mother's accidental death.

Survival in such conditions, especially for a woman, was difficult and she usually dressed as a man and kept to herself. It is during one of her many trips across the States she met with coin engraver hoboes. The hobo nickel is a sculptural form consisting of engraving existing coins.

The buffalo nickel, issued in 1913, was the preferred material as it was thick, softer than other alloy coins and designs of both sides (a buffalo and the big Native American Indian face took almost the whole space from which to carve a smaller face or skull). Monika is often considered as one of the best, alongside more famous carvers such as Bertram Wiegand or George Washington Hughes and her work is sought after by collectors.

Contrary to most hobo engravers Monika only ever carved self-portraits, using a double mirror to see her profile. The coins therefore follow her own ageing. The earliest coins shows her in her mid-twenties. When she passed away in 2004 aged 78, four coins of recent portraits were found in her pockets. More than 50 versions of her profile are known to exist although no collectors possess more than 30. This collection is made even more extraordinary by the fact there are no known photographs of Monika.

Queen Elizabeth II from the United Kingdom was, coincidentally, born one day after Monika Gorniak. Her ageing portrait is on all coins since 1953 although only five versions were ever officially drawn.

Long live queen Monika.

Navid Nuur pressed coin

A 1p coin pressed through a vending machine made by Dutch artist Navid Nuur placed at Parasol Unit in London is not quite the same as a a 1p coin pressed through a vending machine made by Dutch artist Navid Nuur placed at the Stedelijk Museum in Amsterdam because in London one would pay £1 and use a 1p coin as the raw material on which the fingerprint is cheekily pressed and in Amsterdam the cost dramatically drops to €1.01.

ICA pin badge

ICA is a ubiquitous supermarket in Sweden, pronounced 'ee-kah'. The ICA in London is the Institute of Contemporary Arts, pronounced 'eye-cee-ay'. Two institutions in their own right separated by their respective activities and geography. I've never seen ICA outside of Sweden or Norway and there are no reasons to consider the ICA as a true temple of contemporary art without having lived in London and obviously being more than remotely interested in the subject. As someone for whom both references are important, the linking of the two is obvious and ludicrous. Consequently I believed the connection was inevitable, creating an internal chuckle.

The logo of the supermarket is of importance for its sophisticated and stylish linking of the 'C' and 'A' — both beautiful and over present, something a cold, cool, black rimmed glasses turtleneck contemporary art institution would never go for, opting for an over-the-top self-deprecating stance if you were Swiss or more likely post-industrial brutalism for the rest of the western world.

The rest of the world so far has followed US/European aesthetics. Ee-kah on the other hand seems to be a misplaced nineties mistake but it was designed in 1964 by Rune Monö, primarily an industrial designer. If longevity is a testament to anything the creation has survived its author who passed away in 2007 and despite minor changes remains the same in its fifth decade.

I was hoping to cheerily create such geeky empathy when I acquired supermarket bags from Sweden to bring to London and hang out nonchalantly at the ICA. After trying to get someone's attention for half an hour I forgot about it, focusing rather on the exhibition, when I recognised Jens Hoffman, a well-known American curator who had been appointed recently at the helm of the ICA's exhibitions. He was surrounded by two or three people, talking to them with excitement when he interrupted himself looking at my bag and exploding into laughter: 'We should definitely take this as our LOGO!' before disappearing into the gallery with his colleagues, who found the joke hilarious.

I'm at the fishmongers and it dawns on me that I need to finish this book, that the stories of the items contained in my wallet must be consigned elsewhere because the horse carriage they travel on will soon inevitably be replaced by the high speed underground unmanned vehicle of the future that is already here and efficiency doesn't hold much narrative luggage. Soon, no one will use a wallet and already the sometimes non-vegan leathery pouch for the trouser pocket is an antiquity to millennials. Already jeggings — that strange hybrid of jeans and leggings — don't have pockets, only pretend they do.

Rewind to a grey morning at the fishmongers — visiting is a favourite activity of mine, only second to actually cooking and eating the briny waterworld offerings. I scrutinise the gloss of the scaled skins, the eyes, the rainbow shine only the freshest mackerel wear and the gills. Every sense, from the smell to the important goo that you touch to know the state of the fish, is important. The product's fluctuating price can be a sign of how close your urban retailer is from the actual sea. It was in this ultimately analogue environment that I was unexpectedly reminded of the near-obsolescence of my wallet, of its inconvenience at deforming my pocket, the heavyweight reminder of using exact change to alleviate oneself physically and the slight compulsive disorder to pay the exact sum requested in a shop, hoping the coin compartment might miraculously match the price of the acquired item to the penny. This overweight wallet pushes inward against my leg, reassuring me that yes, I am safe, whatever happens I will be able to get home or indulge in an unplanned purchase — the capitalist warranty of controlled freedom.

The fishmonger typed a few numbers on the electronic scale from which the tail fin of my John Dory was dangling and after handing me the 100% recyclable plastic bag containing the delicious délicatesse I could eat raw, presented me the card machine in a ritual that called me to tap my card or phone to magically transfer funds from bank account to bank account, the terrestrial dance of mortals like us while the digital transfer of data is what happens on Olympus.

The fishmonger, Dan, knows me. Not my name nor the rest of me outside of his space but me buying fish. We chat about fish, never about anything else and I doubt I could recognise him if I ever saw him dancing in a club, not surrounded by mussels or gurnards. Our thing is the fish, its origin, what is fresh, how to clean it and eventually the money exchange: metal for flesh, copper for bones. Recently this has changed. What used to be reminiscent of thousands of years of trade between a hungry human with cash and a fishmonger has jumped into the twenty-first century and he has many times been incredulously standing there with an electronic device while I had paper or metal money in my hand.

Me, a monkey in front of a slick, black ageless monolith signalling my upcoming extinction... unless I adapt, unless I agree to let go of my handicapped companion, that I ditch it entirely as there is no upgrade to the wallet. The object and its content have to disappear into the ether of the digital cloud. Exit the Visa cards, the business cards, the coins and even the photos of loved ones, all magically turned into zeroes and ones into a device we still call a phone that is everything else but.

In Alex Proyas's science fiction movie *I, Robot* (2004) there is a scene in which the character played by Will Smith pays for his drink by swiping his wallet onto a round plastic verruca on the counter. It is quick but I could feel the editorial decision of showing this to us as a signifier of a crazy future when money has disappeared physically.

Much like the flatscreen from François Truffaut's *Fahrenheit 451* (1966), the wallet swiping device has almost immediately been outdated by their becoming a banality in our lives. *I, Robot* was right that we'd swipe to pay but was wrong that it would still be a wallet. It would be possible to keep a wallet for its

things and change sim cards on phones. This might be the new Swiss army knife and you can even carry it on a plane.

I'm ashamed to tell of the stress I encountered in Mexico when my phone refused to charge despite contraptions pressing the charger one way or the other, of twisting and holding the cable in a certain way providing precious seconds of battery. Eventually I did seek out professional advice and went to a shop, distressed that I would not be human or part of society without it, especially as I was so far away from home. The seller explained to me that if it didn't charge my phone would be as useless as a brick, prompting rash decision-making, almost immediately purchasing a new one for £700 cash, as if this was the only way to get out of a life-threatening situation. I was so powerless I didn't argue the value and potential of a single brick with him. It was a lot of money but I urgently used my last battery time to Google why it wasn't charging and out of the dozens of solved similar questions none worked so I decided to buy a new one — I mean, why not, I was at rock bottom.

At the very last moment the only rational part of me left, diminishing at high speed, decided to wait until after the next meeting with a friend I hadn't seen for years.

I was unable to express anything other than my petty privileged life tragedy. My friend listened patiently. He was accompanied by a gentleman of an age and fashion that placed him outside of my preconceptions. He was a smiley old man who could be a tramp or a dandy, and I concluded 'both' in my mind. I noticed that he was eyeing my wallet, which I had left open on the table, and I started to worry but was unable to put it back into my pocket without displaying my prejudices. I broke a sweat, a huge drop falling from my forehead as his hand reached for the wallet. He grabbed the red paperclip, twisted it and took my phone, inserted the clip in the charging hole to extract what usually comes out of a gagging cat: a huge hair ball. No words were exchanged but the phone worked like new.

Unused concert ticket
which on closer inspection is a
flyer for an exhibition

Don't you hate it when someone says they're not a curator just before they proceed to tell you about the exhibition they've curated? A sense of modesty sometimes means they use the past-participle verb 'organised' instead of 'curated'. True, everyone curates these days: a 'DJ' curates the music in a pub, a stylist curates a celebrity's wardrobe.

I'm no curator but I couldn't help noticing an open call that appeared in my inbox in 2011. I've never quite been interested in open calls as I prefer to be busy with small projects rather than face the humiliation of rejection. On this occasion, however, something caught my eye and I gave myself an hour to come up with a proposal. The open call came from an association of two Belgian institutions I had never heard of: Z33, Hasselt and Frans Masereel Centrum in Kasterlee. I checked Google Maps and, yes, those were in the middle of regions I didn't know (although at the time my knowledge of Belgium was limited to Brussels). What intrigued me was that this was an open call for an exhibition about graphic arts.

I'd studied graphic design in a course called Communication, Art and Design which, by its own denomination, authorised a service design to step into art.

My practice had ever since been walking the fine line of not being too fine arts as well as a wariness of service and subservience to a client and the power of HIS money. Many years after graduation I was told I misunderstood the title of the course and that there never was a comma between 'Communication' and 'Art'.

This confusion echoed with my reading of the open call and I hastily sent an exhibition proposal for a graphic design show, unbeknown to me that graphic arts has nothing to do with graphic design and is a branch of printmaking. I nevertheless received a positive response and was invited to Hasselt, alongside two other candidates, to an interview for which I was to prepare a more detailed description of the project. Despite the joy of having been shortlisted I quickly realised the task ahead and doubted whether I could write more than a bold one-page proposal — a task for which I was out of my depth as I'm not a curator.

I consulted my partners and decided to cancel the trip. Surely I could, instead, send a bold one-page explanation as to why. The train ticket was already bought and a sense of guilt I had not felt since passing my driving licence test prevented me from sleeping. I was exhausted when the morning came but I had come to my senses and manned up to suffer the consequences: I would go there and when it was my turn, spend my allocated time pleading guilty of having chewed more than I was able to cook, serve and swallow. To my surprise the other two candidates, who seemed extremely confident to me, stayed in the room for my presentation and so did I for theirs. Being the last to be interviewed I shrank in my chair as I listened to the other proposals, well prepared and written, no doubt by people who had curated before. My turn came and one of the characters that lives in my head luckily took over and instead of what would have been a painful confession to why I was keeping on wasting everyone's time my hand went into my pocket and reached for my wallet.

Without explanation I started giving a guided tour of the wallet museum. My logic was that I became a magician who transformed a scary panel into a friendly audience of a guided tour. Every now and then I would wake up from the monologue utterly conscious of how far what was happening was counter to their expectations. I was impressed by their politeness as none of them interrupted me, even if they couldn't hide their surprise.

After 40 minutes or so I decided the tour was over and sat down, attempting a last lame joke: 'If you liked the guided tour I accept tips,' to which they smiled but no laughter nor applause.

I had been caught out for not having prepared for something important but there was a feeling that I still pulled the sympathy card and allowed myself to join them for a drink thereafter. Everyone was much more relaxed and we parted after a few beers. I went back to London, half satisfied that at least there was a story to tell. A few days later I received a phone call from the director of Frans Masereel Centrum, Sofie Dederen, who congratulated me and almost in the same breadth asked: 'So how do you see this guided tour becoming an exhibition?'

I had no idea but I apparently won the open call. I am no curator.

A pound coin, pierced with a hole
and attached to a string

I spent three months studying abroad in London during my bachelor degree. I arrived in the United Kingdom from Paris with an unhealthy fascination for the grim aesthetic of its music from the seventies and eighties and the onscreen toughness in the films of Mike Leigh and Alan Clarke. On the other side of the channel — so close yet so far — a decade of Mitterrand socialism had created a very different atmosphere to Thatcherite conservatism.

England and London looked bleak from this side and somehow still was in the late nineties when I brought a small suitcase to experience short-term study at Central Saint Martins. What I could afford was in Catford, a place I came to become fond of every time I would evoke it to anyone, eyebrows raised, forming a silent 'Why?' as a response to the inevitable question 'Where do you live?' Most people had never been there but would be aware of the big cat statue at the entrance of a sad shopping mall which Japanese people would call 'shutter street' as most of the shops had not opened since the eighties.

The flat was old and carpeted even in the bathroom (a classic in those days), inevitably fitted with double taps, an ongoing source of wonder for continental europeans who could hardly fathom why such feature of the early ages of plumbery would still be prevalent. A Scottish friend I had a crush on — meaning I was inclined to believe anything she said — claimed it was better than a mixer because you controlled the temperature directly with your own hands, cupping the boiling and quickly mixing it with the freezing, a hand version of some extreme Finish sauna tradition.

I shared the flat with a nice couple, or so I thought. The guy was friendly enough but the girl I only ever heard during their very noisy nights. I understood after a few months that she never was the same person after I saw several women leaving the flat early in the morning while I was eating my newly-discovered porridge (we certainly didn't indulge in porridge in France and as such it became central to my infatuation of anything English).

The most wonderful feature of the apartment was that the electricity was archaically metered in-house by each of the flatmates inserting pound coins into a mechanical device that ticked a loud countdown towards powercut. My Scottish friend claimed it was better because you could control the consumption and if you ran out of coins during the night well so it was to be and perhaps I didn't have to keep too much of my perishable food in the fridge. I, again, was convinced of the direct relation between fighting consumerism and the fitting by a national energy provider installing a mechanical device from the nineteenth century in Zone 3 homes.

One evening I noticed a string coming out of the coin slot and pulled it. A coin emerged from the machine. Someone had drilled a hole and attached a string to create an infinity pound.

A soft plastic cigarette box
bought in Matsuyama

She was 31 years old and driving. Her mother, the strong matriarch loved by her family as much as feared, was sitting in the back.

She gives her mum directions to where they should meet later. The mother says, 'Wait a sec, I need to write it down, do you have a piece of paper?'

The daughter replies, 'Look in my bag', and as the words come out she breaks a sweat and mentally inventories the content of her bag, associating items with anticipated sharp remarks from her genitor:

'Lipstick — why so red, so signalling, why not more modest?'
'Key — you must have a second lock or third, it is not safe.'
'Mace (absence of) — I'll buy you one, you know how Arabs are.'

In the corner of her eye, she knows before she sees a hand holding a pack of cigarettes and a screeching voice accompanying the dramatic gesture: 'Shall I write on THIS?'

And it hits her. At her age she still smokes secretly.

A pack of cigarettes which on closer inspection
is a pack of playing cards which on closer
inspection is an exhibition catalogue which on
closer inspection is a performance kit

Smoking used to be everywhere. A single generation
ago people smoked on aeroplanes, as testified by
the remnant feature of unused ashtrays embedded
in ninety percent of the international fleet. I still remember the smoking ban in the UK and the memory
loss we all went through of how we could even
spend so much time in an environment that stank of
cigarettes, inside and out of your clothes and bodies,
especially for non-smokers who, in this case, were
the anomalies who would have to comply if they
wanted a social life. I also remember the wave of the
ban across continental Europe, the French laughing at
it, looking down from their high grounds of the obvious link between philosophical and nouvelle vague
intellectualism and smoke inhaling. The French went
quietly accepting that cafés and bars would now
be smoke free immediately. No protests or outcry,
a silent submissive attitude to western globalisation.

Movies and their universes are another thing. Surely
the characters smoke less than they used to when all
cool characters compulsorily smoked and provided
role models. Occasionally the moviemakers show the
products, allowing a glimpse of a packet or perhaps

the distinctive feature of the filter. Just like anything in the parallel universes of films the brands exist but in a version that is either a blatant product placement or a formally equivalent object. Thus the mysterious Smoking Man from *The X-Files* TV series (1993 – 2018, created by Chris Carter) always had a pack of Morley, an obvious and heavy-handed nod to Marlboro. When the similarities are such, the motivations are questionable.

My design for the catalogue of 'All the Knives' at Z33 in Hasselt (2013) bears a resemblance to a Marlboro pack of cigarettes, although it would be more accurate to say that that it hints at *Morley* cigarettes, the real fake brands. It omits the name entirely but the red shape alone is unmistakingly a reference. Although very supportive, the director of the art centre in which the exhibition occurred mentioned in passing how this could possibly fall into copyright infringement and a lawsuit from Marlboro would put an end to the distribution of the publication. We looked at each other and silently considered the mega-corporation's morning meeting during which a minor executive mentions having visited a show in continental Europe, in a city that is not even a capital, and buying a catalogue that was made as an edition of 1000. Marlboro could crush the city itself like an insect. We went ahead.

A few years later I was at an airport going through the obligatory route of the duty free goods when I noticed Marlboro's new packet design where the name was not printed but just given a subtle gloss shine, an almost invisible logo, making every single packet look similar to our catalogue. I immediately called Sofie, the above mentioned director of the art centre, and we convened a meeting to consider whether or not we should sue Marlboro for ripping us off.

A 2007 British first-class stamp commemorating Arnold Machin's stamp design, still in use, issued initially in 1967 featuring Queen Elizabeth II. The stamp is tautologically illustrated by the original stamp

Queen Elizabeth II accessed to the throne in 1952 — her reign is a longevity to be reckoned with. She is a public figure people see regularly on television and the internet, making it logical her effigies would be updated as she ages. While coins and banknotes have had designs change over the years the profile on the stamps still show her as a young monarch. This portrait even outlasted the denominations as the stamp had a value of 4d (denarii) based on Roman systems but in 1966 the British decided to convert to a decimal system which other countries had already used for a century or more.

This curious portrait of Dorian Gray comes in red or gold for first class stamps and blue for second class. Even though the classes do represent a value — respectively 70p and 61p as of January 2020 — they are theoretically 'eternal', meaning one could still send a letter with an old stamp as long as it bears the first class denomination. It is a contract and one could see a proof of confidence from the system. Samuel Vermeil, a French graphic designer who used to be part of the graphic design studio M/M Paris showed me a permanent pass for the Palais de Tokyo, issued when the Parisian art centre first opened in 2002 and for which the design studio created a visual identity. He has not used the pass for fifteen years and cannot vouch for the validity.

Most postal systems offer a new service that allows consumers to design their own stamp. This was made possible by the democratisation of digital printing and it is often used to personalise invitations to weddings or the announcement of a birth, even if it might spoil the ritualistic surprise of opening a sealed envelope.

The chocolate brand M&M's also offers a similar personalised service: an image or a word can be printed on each chocolate pill for a modest sum. As of 2013, it was possible to get 'A DRUG' printed on them.

The American civil war lasted four years, from 1861 to 1865. It divided the north and the south pointedly on the issue of African American slavery. I came across this coin in a museum shop in Minneapolis. I do not recall the museum itself but was excited to be able to buy this dark souvenir, a replica of a coin minted by the Confederate government — AKA the bad guys who, fortunately, lost the war.

At first I was disgusted and fascinated at the bold-ness of representing tobacco and cotton on one side but also a chain, which I believed to be an arrogant pro-slavery symbol. Apparently the chain is what links the secessionist states and the missing letters in the last four links are meant to be an invitation for other states to join them. This immediately remind-ed me of a mixed feeling I experienced when I saw a contemporary Arabic copy of *Mein Kampf* in a Moroccan bookstore. I could not, however, find it in me to purchase it and let myself be distracted by my own morbid curiosity. Instead I bought another book, also in arabic of *The Motorcycle Diaries* by Che Guevara, two shelves down.

This time I did purchase the coin and my complaint to the cashier is that at $4.95 they just missed the opportunity to sell a $5 coin from the nineteenth century at its real price. He did not find this funny nor did the cashier at the Louvre when I commented that the poster souvenir of Mona Lisa was only a few millimetres smaller than the real one, that it was close but no cigar.

120 mini bricks
from Stacey's Miniature Masonry, scale 1:24
that can be laid out like real bricks,
designed especially for doll's houses or miniature
train dioramas.

The guided tour of this wallet could last anything between five minutes to an hour and a half, depending on the comfort of the place where the items contained within the wallet could be laid out and the enthusiasm or lack of expressed by the visitor(s).

The collection itself started from the observation that some items we take for granted would have other stories to tell than the pure functionality we carry them for. Once I had accumulated enough of those the idea of a guided tour came as an alternative to creating a museum for which one would have to establish a communication strategy to get an audience. With The Knife, the museum would instead go to the visitors and one by one we could perhaps reach a reasonable attendance to this exhibition.

The versatility was great in theory but the attention span of a stranger who had been drinking five pints in a pub is always different to the stiff, yet prepared visitor to an art exhibition. After a while, and only if two of us would present the collection, we decided one would take 120 bricks out of one's pocket and slowly but surely recreate a sculpture by Carl

Andre (*Equivalent VIII*, 1966, an arrangement of 120 firebricks on the floor of the gallery) as both a side performance to the guided tour but also as a way to keep time. It wouldn't be as abrupt as an alarm clock but it proved to be a good amount of time and if they wanted to hear more we would continue as a successions of encores.

A
¥1000
banknote
folded to show
an eye at the top of a pyramid

What exactly isn't possible to prove by the clever application of origami to a banknote? Most conspiracy theorists only forward and convey information found on the internet or earlier in self-published books. I often find myself in awe of the ones who discover things like a millimetre-wide owl on a coin or on the top of a skyscraper. How different, really, are they from an observant artist?

While picking up my daughter from school a parent friend approached me. He is a charming father of two, a director of photography for TV, cinema and high profile artists. I enjoy our conversations a lot and we keep on trying to work together. The failure to create the necessary budget from my side has prevented the collaboration but we maintain the possibility as I am also fascinated to see how a professional handles things one usually botches for lack of money. Once he told me about filming onboard refugee rescue boats. His account of the feeling of fear still gives me goosebumps and a sense of powerlessness in face of the disasters some people find courage to live through. Being told the story while drinking a cappuccino in an area we both helped gentrify makes the sword of guilt clearly appear above us.

Anyway, this friend came up to me at school, slightly complaining about the lack of work around and one thing led to another, I mentioned not reading the newspaper anymore and I only get glimpses of the horror on TV screens at airports, muted but always subtitled on CNN as I travel quite a bit. The conversation suddenly turned into a monologue from his part on media control and before I could make light jokes he confirmed The World Trade Center and the 9/11 attacks to be an American operation. I was taken aback but did I not understand we were in the virtual world of pretence between two friends inventing improbable scenarios for our own entertainment?

I then proceeded to mention the burning of the Reichstag by Adolf Hitler as a precedent to covert operations. He didn't quite let me finish and continued to describe what I then felt was serious and that he did believe it. For sure the recent years have been shaking institutions and belief systems, some for the better, decentralising everything from the western white-centric power structure but being told about conspiracies at 8am in a school playground was disturbing. There is no doubt he has none. I went home puzzled.

A torn out Marlboro cigarette pack

Jochen Dehn gave me this piece of rubbish treasure. He is a master storyteller and I knew there would be something special when he assumed his narrative voice while handing me this old piece of card which came out of his wallet. This is an electronic key to a major institution in Paris, he said. A high security museum with most artefacts under heavy triple-thickness glass vitrines and an invigilator every five metres, he added.

He had been invited to exhibit at the said museum and somehow got himself locked after-hours despite having been warned the place shut down after all employees left. Artists can have quite different working hours but here mostly would have to conform to other people's schedule. I must emphasise Jochen, if given a choice between the comfortable and the difficult would usually prefer the latter situation which widened the spectrum of habits and what is commonly unquestionable.

My first encounter with Jochen occurred on the island of Capri, stranded with a bunch of artists in low season of the island near Naples. None of us had visited the place but we knew two things: it is very touristic in the summer and the island was the location of Casa Malaparte where Jean-Luc Godard famously shot *Le Mépris* (1963). For a curator to bring ten artists with the only aim to create a collaborative work without preparation stretched egos and the brief communal living was a challenge to the nerves of all.

Inviting artists and specifically mentioning there would be no pressure to produce anything is the best way to produce the very pressure to do so. One evening we discussed at length the Godard villa, recently restored after years of being abandoned. The fame afforded by the sixties movie didn't suffice to save the villa from becoming a ruin and only recently had it been acquired by a private foundation that fenced it off even though it was already difficult to access, being mostly surrounded by sea and a rather dangerously decayed footpath. Alcohol and artistic bravados helping, we decided to organise a mission to go and see it anyhow.

Jochen was the very convincing captain to the expedition. Some of us declined, refusing to do something as obviously illegal as trespassing on private property. Jochen simply said he had something in his bag which would solve any problems encountered. I was fascinated by the idea art would be a force to rival ethics and the law and somehow convinced my partner we should go with our daughter, then still a baby who we'd have to carry (with time I came to realise how inconsiderate I had been but I somehow believed that our daughter could not pass the perhaps unique experience of feeling the infra-thin remnant of Godard's passage and the aura generated by poetry impregnating a piece of architecture).

I had not seen my partner so distraught when she decided to stay and she watched us leave. At first it was exciting to rediscover paths half-hidden by nature but there was a passage on a cliff which made me realise that the physical danger was real. A visceral and animal instinct told me I could not continue and reluctantly went back as I could see we were close enough to see the famous red walls and the staircase of Casa Malaparte, only separated by the third barbed wire fence we had encountered. When I returned I could see relief but also anger in my partner's eyes. I could only silently admit I was wrong.

A few hours later, the last three adventurers returned. It was already dark and we all were waiting to hear what had happened. The thickness of tension, between excitement and nausea, had made us all silent. As they entered, some of us unconvincingly cheered, inviting them to tell us. I still remember the look in their eyes which would and should have been one of victory but instead they had mentally joined us in our melancholia. They kept the silence about the episode ever since. Over time fragments of the story emerged, such as the encounter with two people in the villa, the incongruous offering by Jochen of his secret weapon of love in his bag, the following broken English conversation, the palpable fear and discomfort that such meeting should not take place, the limits to why art is a different word from life.

All of this came back as a flash when Jochen gave me this piece of card many years later. He told me of how being alone in the darkness of the museum he thought of the options, one being spending the night and be discovered the next day by agents of security, another one to force his way out, in what could be a breakout worth telling. After an hour of pondering if it was safe to even walk around when aware that such place would have cameras and alarms a cleaner appeared and casually spoke to him about this involuntary incarceration. She then pulled out a pack of cigarettes from her pocket and fashioned an indented card from it, similar to the one Jochen had given me. This opens the doors, she said, and Jochen got out using it.

Harriet Tubman $20 bill

Under Barack Obama's presidency in 2016, the secretary of the treasury made public the decision that Harriet Tubman would be the new figure on the $20 bill. It is commonly thought that she would take the place of Andrew Jackson but the announcement was that he would be moved to the back, thus replacing the White House (people versus architecture — one – nil). Harriett on one side, Jackson on the other.

Andrew Jackson has figured on the banknote since 1928. The seventh president of the United States was known to be against federal money and even warned 'the people' during his final address against paper money. His presence on the $20 for almost a century might be an elaborate joke by the US Department of the Treasury. We will never know as, according to the Frequently Asked Questions of the Treasury website, 'Treasury Department records do not reveal the reason that portraits of these particular statesmen were chosen in preference to those of other persons of equal importance and prominence'.

If one focuses on the negative, Jackson was also a wealthy slave and plantation owner and his presence on the obverse of Harriet Tubman makes for a small albeit late posthumous victory for the abolitionist. Harriet Tubman was born a slave and later in her activist work was instrumental in the long struggle against discrimination. It is arguable whether her appearance on money is the relevant consecration she deserves but it is a start. Or, it was a start until the Trump administration halted the redesign which was to take place in 2020.

Dano Wall, a designer from New York not satisfied with the indefinite postponement, decided to act upon it. 'I am', he wrote, 'disappointed by the news that the Trump administration was walking back the plan to put Harriet Tubman on the $20 bill'. Instead, he created a stamp to convert the figure of Jackson into Tubmans. Dano makes available the files of the stamp if you can access 3D printing and engraving or one can acquire the stamp directly from him to change every banknote, one at a time. Though anti-counterfeiting laws prohibit the wilful destruction of, and stamping of advertisements upon, paper money, pursuant to 1.1.18 U.S.C. § 333 of the United States Code, stamped currency is fit for circulation so long as its denomination remains legible.

100 Swedish krona, featuring
Carl Linnaeus,
the father of modern taxonomy

My creationist friend agreed not to use a 100 krona banknote whenever he was in Sweden. In return, I promised I would only ever use the $20 bill with Harriet Tubman on it.

A piece of paper
that a child of five wrote to her father
claiming he is the best dad she ever had

Is it socially acceptable for a father to not have a picture of his daughter as his main screensaver? I am wondering this for the first time as it never occurred to me not to, despite being someone who, before my own child, sighed every time I saw this on someone else's phone. Is it also true that one naturally thinks their child is the most beautiful in the world when some photographs prove otherwise and allow some distance to criticality? Look at her and find she is the most beautiful in the flesh, turn to the photo when she was a baby looking like a David Lynch character in black and white. Both are real. I carry this note but try to avoid showing it to people, even though I am telling you about it right now, my unfortunate reader.

A few years back I wrote a short story for a Japanese magazine. In the story I imagined an altercation with my daughter in the future, ten years to be exact. It is titled 'Dad, you cunt'. There goes a word I had never said but I took pleasure in writing it to a Japanese audience that would have pixelated the word if it was an image. It went like this, slightly edited:

'You cunt! A fucking embarrassment,' she screamed, slamming the door.

My 14-year-old daughter has just called me a cunt. I'm standing in her bedroom and the feeling of vertigo hits: I recognise that I'm in a clichéd situation, albeit one so violent that no movie could have prepared me for. My head spins and I go back in time, to more than ten years ago when I was in this very same room, making a list of Luna's possessions, if we could call them that, considering she didn't choose most of the toys littered in her space that she'd later designate private and off limits to her parents only a few years later.

On my list I divided the objects into categories:

Books (96)
The logic was that since she'd naturally speak four languages, acquired from her parents and grand-parents, she should have books in each language. As book collectors, we also smuggled in Romanian, Mexican and Korean books that we didn't understand, but enjoyed the images of, hoping she'd share our interest for printed matter. The irony was, of course, that over the classic Munari books, she'd prefer the glossy magazines of Peppa Pig, an annoyingly posh know-it-all of a pig.

Soft toys (49)
I'd bought an alien facehugger soft toy from For-bidden Planet, the geek palace I would still indulge in visiting until my mid-forties. A baby was the perfect

alibi to buy the adult toys. In the beginning, her natural instincts made her wary of this parasite that lay eggs in humans who later explode, giving birth to an almost invincible Alien with acid blood. Equally she hated the Freddy Krueger toy and, considering he was a child molester, it was absolutely fair enough.

Wooden objects (41)

Exquisitely crafted spinning tops in endangered wood were treated in the same way as sticks picked from the nearby park. We also had a wooden rainbow she ignored, as if in the knowledge they were just for Monocle reading design-conscious parents.

Plastic toys (437 including broken bits)

Playmobil and LEGO are classics. Playmobil females are just male Playmobil with added breasts (Michelangelo did that, right?).

Musical instruments and records (11)

Years of brainwashing her with Joy Division and Sonic Youth in the hope she might develop a punk mentality were not wasted if we consider the way she consciously flipped her finger at me as early as when she turned eight years old.

DVDs (26)

The usual suspects, plus some experimental pop video compilation from The Residents. She was never frightened by them.

Dolls' houses (3)
Strangely she wouldn't mix the different toys so much.
Animals with animals, Playmobil with Playmobil, and
characters from different animations would never
really cross over.

Home-made toys (13)
The pride of a parent-child relationship in the face of
toy corporations. We would make more and more
of those. Her godfather would tell me: 'you have to
buy her some real toys too.'

iPad (1)
She was always surprised that laptops didn't have
touch screens.

Artworks and editions (34)
She played with Lawrence Weiner wood blocks,
had Martin Creed hand-painted T-shirts (sporting the
number 27 — the age rock stars died), dried herself
with a Peter Doig towel, as well as many presents from
all the artists she met. She saw her first performance
when she was three weeks old, farting an amount
of gas her small body could not possibly contain in
the first seconds of some brilliant intervention by
Bedwyr Williams.

We had planted the seeds of her rebellion and, on
her twelfth birthday, she claimed she wanted to become a banker.

I went after her to apologise.

***

I publicly read this in a talk and while I was doing so
realised a dear friend was in the audience. His job
had, for most of his life, been related to law, finance
and banking — I never quite understood the details.
I knew my text and what was coming. The arro-
gance of the final remark, as well as the obviousness
of the artist-banker dichotomy, was a dire banality.
I disgracefully escaped the discomfort by replacing
'banker' by 'insert here the worst job you can think
of as a father for your daughter to embrace'.

A CHF 10 banknote featuring Le Corbusier

Say what you will about modernism but it is both revered and reviled in equal measures, often by the same people. In this instance of the frozen portrait on the Swiss banknote, Le Corbusier is portrayed in a movement that is less statuesque than the usual stern eternal pose. He is shown in the moment after he put his classic glasses up but his hand is still holding them. What seems casual is to me an even more reprobative gesture from an elder. You may remember this look on a usually posh older person who pulls down their glasses to look at you or rather your death metal t-shirt or skirt they deem too short. That's the one that says 'tssk', yes the banknote comes with a sound of disappointment and makes me feel I am 13 years old again.

Bastard.

A 4 colour BIC pen that on closer inspection contains only the colour blue

A classic of cheap, the BIC pen is the pride of French industry. Everybody's got one, especially around me. None of us have ever finished more than one of the four regular colours — blue, black, red and green — and when that does happen, usually the black, it becomes useless. Writing in blue reminds me of school, where we used green to correct our own mistakes while the teachers would use the more aggressive red.

We still love it, perhaps not the four colour pen that has an orange body, indicating the thin ball pen, too screechy on paper, better the blue, fatter, smoother, rolling nicely from the finger to the pen to the tip to the paper. For this specific one I bought four 4 colour BICs and replaced one of them with blue inks and blue indicators only, naively satisfied by the tautology, ignoring the other three pen which I didn't quite like because the body of the pen was blue and not black or green or red. A few years later Saâdane Afif made a 4 colour BIC in black, body included, for Lafayette Anticipations, the private art foundation.

Of course, I believed he'd ripped me off, jealous that he actually worked with the company and that his was widely distributed and known. To be fair it is generally true of his work compared to mine. Ultimately and that is the most important: it was not really the same idea.

Thoughts about Brixton: Very far south of east London where all your friends live. An eventful night of seeing a fat-made mountain installation in a cinema lobby just before watching a brilliant slow movie by Matthew Barney, falling in and out of slumber, reassured by the fact not much had happened in between and puzzled by the mystery of it all. Yes, it is allowed to do things like this. Another night at the Brixton Academy, a legendary concert venue to see The Pixies a lifetime after having made them the soundtrack of a younger life. There is a magic show by the drummer who had given up punk rock until this reunion. Everyone around is old, the smiles are young, the bellies are tired. How can one be so happy and disappointed in equal measures? Was I there or did I watch the documentary? Was it The Pixies or Teenage Fanclub at the Hippodrome? The latter but the feelings are the same. Was it the same night, yet another party that finishes on the wooden floor, inebriated to the brim and unable to face the three successive night buses to the way of one's own bed. This time the warmth of a classmate who later would move to Berlin and would not really change except the few wrinkles around the beautiful eyes that laugh and oh yes, a child and a proper job, kind of. Another day in Brixton Market moaning with a friend about gentrification and how it used to be good, the smelly fish one wouldn't dream of buying, the bric à brac and the fear at night. Then the latest, a trip to buy money as Brixton has its own, presumably to keep it circulating within an analogue mile with shops in the neighbourhood accepting it at face value and what faces: Olive Morris or Bowie, Luol Deng and Violette Szabo as well as stylised landmarks of the area. Went there, bought some, came back east, gave half, kept the other, away from circulation, away from the purpose of its creation. Partially satisfied, partially conned.

I usually present this as a fake 10p coin, which does get laughter at the obvious crassness of the realisation. However, a lot of care has gone into making it and it could be fair to claim a higher value, this being made by hand and unique, glazed and therefore requiring a biscuit firing. Counterfeiters probably aim at making money fast and on the very edge of functionality, good enough to be but never spend more time or money that would cancel the very essence of making fake money. The art of forgery is celebrated when heroes of World War II made perfect passports to save lives but money forgery for personal gain simply appears as the lowest of jobs.

This very coin being in ceramics creates the fear in me that it is too delicate to join the crowd or even my own wallet. It sits between two cards. Like a protective parent I dread for it the company of other tough coins in different alloys, specifically designed to accommodate a promiscuous life of greasy finger manipulation and rubbing each other in the confines of a small pocket, pouch, wallet, plastic zipper-locked bag, the transparency of which is compromised by the hard edges and dirt. Not my baby. The wrong material, definitely too fragile for this world.

Recently the paper money in the UK was changed to a thin plastic material, some parts left unprinted and see through. My mother, despite having seen other currencies in this material in other countries, suddenly forgot it ever existed elsewhere and questioned its authenticity at a grocery store, looking suspiciously at the cashier while a long queue of customers politely fumed at her. 'Is this real?' she asked the merchant who was almost too young to have known paper money, a confusion duel was about to take place. I sometimes use my own homemade fake money, less as a prank, more as a desperate attempt to create an audience for something I've made, possibly the exact opposite of what a counterfeiter would aspire to. The reactions are usually one of surprise and a smile follows unless it reminds them that the whimsicality of making such objects accentuates their own suffering at doing a job they hate and resent.

A bitcoin coin

You heard the story too, not this one exactly but exactly the same one. He was a little maverick, a hacker of sorts, nothing too dodgy, mostly a genius according to his enthusiastic friends. He worked with this guy, you know, this guy who was in cryptocurrency a long time ago when nobody knew what it was. He was clever, that computer friend and he could see something was happening. Instead of taking the little cash there was he agreed on money that only existed digitally. He knew this was anyhow mostly the case in the world since Nixon unlinked the dollar with the available gold to take control of the world when America could have gone bankrupt. He knew that well and anyway worst come to worst he would lose 200 euros, barely a fraction of rent and zooming out, he could see the bigger picture. He then agreed on the handshake and an email as a contract. The rest is history, as they say, as he managed to hold on to the bitcoins until the multiplication factor became absurd, just a number on a screen that got bigger because of people's beliefs. It grew and grew, until everyone got onto this. Even your grandmother knew what a bitcoin was, a sign the time was up. He jumped the sinking boat to buy a house where he lives today, in the middle of Paris, he isn't 30 yet. You've heard the story. All I could do about this was to buy a bitcoin coin on eBay. It came from China by post. It was in metal with a design that referenced the digital world. I was happy to own an aberration but strongly felt conned. I am the opposite of that guy.

I saw Samuel from a distance, accompanying his son August on a blue scooter. He is a dad from school where my son goes and we sometimes chitchat, trying to suss out if we can become friends, both mentally imagining whether speaking to each other would happen if our progeniture didn't exist. My opinion was that we wouldn't, even if I appreciated the conversations that continued over a coffee after drop off. We carefully chose the subjects of conversation to be interesting enough but never too revealing. We are both divorced and trying to not make this the cement that binds a potential friendship. I like August because he's got the same hairstyle as Johnny Ramone, except he is blonde and 63 years younger than the rockstar.

There is an unspoken rule in the playground between separated parents which is legion: we only talk about ex-partners, if ever, in positive terms. Even when the war seems to be on, the schoolyard forces truce and you don't recruit your army for later. Parents are possibly superstitious and the negative waves are kept at bay from the children.

I could see something was up as Samuel is French and cannot quite contain his emotions. He smiled at me, as we waved goodbye to our kids. 'Can we have coffee?' he asked, although it was more of a

218

statement. I had boasted about how free I was given my job so it was difficult to refuse. As we sat down he immediately spoke of a recent fight with his ex regarding August's hairstyle. Last weekend, August complained about his fringe being too long and Samuel had snipped some hair. Armed with the scissors he felt confident that the front rearrangement should be met with side waves of blonde flocks. It quickly appeared to him that hairdressers were not just randomly cutting hair but had a knowledge of three-dimensional space and the way different hair reacts to gravity and the form of a skull.

'I stopped before I did too much damage but it was fine overall,' he said, before immediately adding, 'Then it was time to get August to Sandra. When we got to her flat she almost instantly screamed at me about the hair.' 'What have you done?!' she screeched. 'Man that was intense,' he concluded, shaken by the memory. I shivered. This was familiar. Last year I also felt this silly confidence of being gifted in a field I had no skills for, coiffuring. My son, a cute four-year old who looks good in any clothes, like most kids, and has the nonchalence of a rockstar, had been watching some videos of Die Antwoord, a band with attitude but also radical hairdos. Ninja, the singer, has his sides shaven and most definitely is ugly-beautiful. A wind of insanity gushed into my brain and I decided to give my son the same hairstyle as a response to his liking of the music. He looked extremely cute and my closest friends were speechless, which I took for the admiration one feels when confronted with an artwork. These were signs I did not identify and I brought him to school on Monday morning for his week with his mother.

We get along and even sometimes work together, trying to be the best parents ever. This week I was to be in Paris for work and after drop-off went straight to the Eurostar. At exactly 6.30pm the angry mother called me as I was cycling down the Seine river banks. At first I thought something had happened and tried to calm her down. It quickly appeared that the upset was the hairstyle which I had completely forgotten but also was proud of, even possibly awaiting some compliments from her. Boy was I off the mark by the longest shot. This was interpreted as the most aggressive attack on the peaceful post break-up re-construction we had both been working on. The next twenty minutes were so violent and on the edge that it came to a very significant moment which I still remember as a very clear changing life moment, an important crossroad that, in a flash, made me under-stand why there were wars.

In the heated conversation that just went exponen-tially up, a sentence formed in my mind and almost

220

exactly simultaneously as it was going to come out I realised that if it did, things would never be the same, that it could never be unsaid, never forgotten, never forgiven and the rest of our shattered lives would find its origin within those very words. Time stood still and I was lucky to realise this and decided in a spilt second I would not detonate the bomb. It took another twenty minutes of discussion to clear the red situation to an acceptable blue that has prevailed ever since. During the cold war, when both the Russians and the Americans were one button away from destroying each other and everyone, the situation had an acronym: Mutually Assured Destruction — M.A.D. I told Samuel about this and concluded: Don't touch the hair, man. Don't touch the hair.

He nodded silently.

The value of time. Time spent on the phone, sang the band MGMT, time spent on video games, time spent being angry. Time spent writing this, time spent reading it. Is time really money? The answer is no, always, you can double-check.

This coin is a token of time spent with a friend for several days 'instead of working', as another friend put it in a fairly passive aggressive manner when I told her about it.

This all started when Hannah, the first friend mentioned, announced via the social media channel she took on to professionalise making jewellery from a hobby and pastime of hers. Irony ensued and I couldn't help sending a video of Portlandia, a spoof comedy about the preconceptions that Portland in Oregon was the hipsterest capital of hipsters of the western world. In the short video, someone who constantly changed interests and jobs is made fun of until she settles for making jewellery. Hannah never responded to the link, nor did her brother-in-law, an alpha male furniture designer to whom I had sent a video of Portlandia featuring a furniture maker as the embodiment of masculinity made fun of. I am pretty sure there must be an episode in which a graphic designer desperately tries to become an artist.

Once I felt safe these were faded memories I contacted Hannah whose work had impressed me since. I wanted to be a fly on the wall to see the magic operate in an attempt to learn something while reconnecting. She had a beautiful shed in which a state of the art jewellery-making set-up was installed, with weird tools, most of which I had never seen and could only imagine the specific use of. While she was crafting a necklace, commenting on the process for me, I made this fake £1 coin in the knowledge we would transform red modelling clay into a bronze spoon/ring/object later in town.

We had a lot of fun, which makes for a rather boring story to read, however I understood this episode of sending her the video was perhaps too close to her own uncertainty about life, especially being surrounded by successful siblings and friends who were fully engaged in careers that were beyond questioning. I do have to come clean and confess this story is published with the hopes that she reads it and forgives me for making public an apology long overdue.

Kajsa and I had just been fired from our teaching job at the Royal College of Art, London when I was approached during a dinner in Reims by a woman wearing sunglasses at night. She introduced herself very vaguely and enquired as to whether I was available to teach in Switzerland, more specifically in Geneva. Knowing the childish feud between Lausanne and Geneva I asked her whether it was okay that I taught at both places. She quickly changed subject and I did not hear from her for the next six months, Autumn passed, winter came and I received a phone call from Alexandra (it is her name and she didn't wear sunglasses in the evenings because she valued herself celestially but because of conjunctivitis) who exclaimed, 'But you do not teach in Lausanne!' to which I concurred.

'I thought you said you did and had given up on hiring you until I realised half a year later this was just a joke.' At the time I had followed the advice of many of the greats by not explaining or refuting what was a funny self-sabotaging situation. Of course I needed the job but I could simply not say the words 'I'm just kidding.'

Out of this misunderstanding began a fruitful collaboration at HEAD for which I love giving workshops, especially with my friend Yaïr Barelli. Our workshop is titled Le Magnifique Avventure and was in 2018 in its seventh year running thanks to Alexandra defending its necessity, even if very little proof that it ever happened — read documentation or presentation — exists. Yaïr and I are not averse to documentation, provided it doesn't destroy the experience itself but every year the students defend the right to keep it as a personal process or at least within the small group of participants.

In the meantime I was also commuting every now and then to Geneva to mentor, tutor or follow student diplomas and had become a regular with a pigeonhole bearing my name. I had, however, noticed I wasn't given a business card which I really wanted because I thought this would give me access to free entries in the world's museums or at least a discounted fee. Every year I begged and every year I was told to be patient. On the seventh year of asking I decided to take the matter into my own hands and use the print-on-demand services that are available and had by then reached an acceptable level of quality. I designed it with all the information that I thought would be required, such as emphasising the ART in the name as design doesn't get you into museums.

The whole thing came in a package 72 hours after uploading it on a website and I was satisfied at the result, taking comfort in the fact that while the cards were fake the situation was real. A week later an email came from the head of the department. They were redesigning their cards so she remembered my asking of one every year. The proposal was thus: I could design the cards for the whole department, be paid for it and also get one for myself. This would render my fake cards obsolete but I believed this action provoked the request in a somewhat irony of destiny or something like that.

It was time for the week-long workshop Le Magnifique Avventure during which we stay together with the students who therefore don't go home for five days, implying we need to find places to sleep and as it is February in Switzerland the cold prohibits improvised urban bivouacking or at least we avoid sleeping in the snow. One night we unanimously (12 students and two tutors) decided it was okay to sleep in a building which did not belong to the school anymore but which some of the students still held the keys for. A good working session, some good karaoke and alcohol induced art ideas, we all slept in different empty rooms of the ex-art college building. Needless to say we got caught and one thing leading to another we got fired from the school. I had designed the cards and they were in production but I wasn't really expecting the school to send me mine. I still have the really fake ones.

Adam and Eve it

We've all done it, the illogical urge to own part of a compelling installation, a sculpture, maybe a painting? Using love to justify theft. You are in Venice, impressed at a cigarette sticking out of a bum. This is a sculpture by Sarah Lucas, the bum is in plaster, the cigarette real. You are loving it. You are a cannibal you must consume and believe part of the brilliance of the soul will be infused into you. You take it, you don't smoke it.

Later you are in the Pompidou Centre and you see a world map made of marbles on the floor. You must consume again so you pick one up. The young invigilator comes and asks you what you did. You tell the truth because stealing is ok, lying isn't. You are somewhat confident. He is not, a red face, unable to articulate words or even feelings as he struggles to barely start to envisage the unlikely possibility that this could ever happen. You feel for him, you feel for the beauty of his belief that he is there merely to enlighten people about the importance of art. He never liked the idea of invigilation, his world is only positive and art is the saviour. He just saw evil enacted, he is changed forever, he mumbles: 'But… why? You… cannot.'

You give him back the marble. The big deal is to discover his faith and it was worth it.

Years later in Belgium in the Koenraad Dedobbeleer
exhibition there's a sculpture of an urn in which there
are coins the artist has defaced, plenty of them, plenty
of stories coming with you, picking them up for your
own benefit, an 'acquisition' for your wallet museum.
The hand is fast. The fingers grab a coin, it lands in
the pocket. Twenty minutes later you have changed
your mind and return to the sculpture, put the coin
back and add one of yours you had just made. Add
insult to injury to plaster on the wrong arm.

A warning message
appearing when trying to scan US currency

You scan a US dollar and this message will appear from the ghost in the machine and the ghost is American: 'This application does not support the editing of banknote images.' You scan euro bills or pound notes and the message will come too, asserting the axis of good western friendship. You scan Singaporean dollars and you can Photoshop at will.

My Scottish friend Sue had mentioned a few times her suffering of what she defined as racism in England. 'But you are the same race', I naively would say. I only just had deciphered that every time she uttered the sound GARRRLLL, which puzzled me for six months, rendering incomprehensible the whole sentence — but oh my, was she pretty — meant 'girl'. Everyone at college liked her and she was very popular. I once confessed to Jason, a pure Australian who sometimes would draw with her that I only understood an average 12% of what she said, that she probably knew and had very likely simplified her vocabulary whenever speaking to me in a not so subtle non-patronising way. I was both hurt and flattered by her gesture. Jason replied, 'I don't understand her, no one does.'

Only a week later I comprehended the situation of being from Scotland in England. Sue and I were out and about for lunch and went into what Brits think a bakery is, where she bought some crisps she would later demonstrate how to crush and sprinkle in an egg and cress sandwich (to the delight of my French cuisine snobbish sensibility). At the till the cashier looked at the Scottish banknote she was handing and in the rudest way snapped, 'What is this?' To which Sue replied, in a well rehearsed manner, 'You'll find this is legal tender.' The cashier shook his head and I swiftly paid while I could see tears of rage in Sue's huge blue eyes. This happened all the time. She was still fuming when we ate our lunch. 'To be fair,' she said, 'the different banks of Scotland issue different designs so even for us, we sometimes don't recognise the money.'

My parents' Japanese passports used to specify that it was valid anywhere in the world except North Korea. As a child this frightened me. What was happening there?

I have the feeling this warning is no longer printed in Japanese passports.

I could swear American soldiers wore skull masks when invading Iraq again. I perfectly recall watching this on TV in a bar that had table football. I even remember the taste of the beer which I since associate with the shocking horror mask tactics. Later, I told the story and was met with incredulity. I checked on the internet and I couldn't find it anywhere.

I am in Tel-Aviv airport, without a belt, without shoes and without a phone or a pen, waiting to be interrogated. My wallet is given back to me after three and a half hours. I check it. Everything is fine except… except they exchanged my Palestinian coins for shekels. I was furious but the constant questioning had worn me and I could just about make it to my plane so I kept my mouth shut. As I am telling this to Yaïr, who I am not blaming personally for being Israeli, he says there isn't such a thing as Palestinian coins. '… Yet,' he adds as a gesture of sympathy.

I am taken aback by my delusion.

A ceramic object in the shape of an iPhone 6

Lying in bed, looking at Myspace, no, Facebook, no, Instagram feeds, checking for notifications, a red dot on apps indicating the world is going on and on, plus letting you know it does, catch up, quick. The auntie who was sitting next to the phone, the landline, checking every now and then that the receiver was properly hung up, just in case. People would call but would hear the occupied tone while she wouldn't hear the call, a major case of miscommunication and neither part wants that. Spending too much time next to the phone, being ready for the call. Never mind, she moved the sofa in the corridor so she could wait comfortably.

Her grandson is luckier, no need to move heavy furniture these days. The phone is small, light and apparently contains more technology than what took humans to the moon and back. Is evolution sometimes backwards? The mobile phone is such a device we will soon forget why it is called a phone. Just like the icon of the camera on motorways, indicating it was designed when Hasselblad and Japanese medium format cameras were around, soon replaced by the pocket-sized compressed portal to everything in life.

Her grandson is not luckier. He inherited a sense of anxiety and insecurity about his place in the world, how he should constantly be on standby for the call, or at least the notification, then the wave, the nudge, the wink, the subconscious sign, anything at all really. His right hand performs a ritual despite his better judgement, tapping his jeans pocket first to the right for the wallet, yes it's there, tapping the left pocket for the phone, yes it's there too. Soon, he taps his forehead, in the name of the father, contactless Mastercard and the holy ghost in the machine. He has to do it because his left thigh is often tingling, vibrating. Last year it started vibrating even when the phone wasn't in the pocket. Of its own will. You got a message, said the thigh.

Age coin

At the front desk of the hotel is a transparent plastic cup usually full of coins. They have a hole in the middle and both sides are identical. It says 'age coin'. In the Netherlands the cigarette vending machines are located in restaurants and hotel lobbies. You swipe your ID card to prove your choice of consumption is mature and legal. Some older vending machines cannot read cards. They swallow coins they assume only adults would have access to, hence a plastic cup at the front desk.

Is it a good idea to give pocket money to kids in order to teach them responsibility, autonomy, or give them a taste of life with money, an inevitable reality? He asked his seven-year-old child, 'Would you rather have regular pocket money or that your mother and I individually buy you stuff?' The child looked up, thinking, as though she were scrutinising the inside of her skull for the best answer. 'Would you buy me anything?' She affirmed more than asked. 'Of course,' double-bluffed the father.

A business card for Jeanne Dielman,
23 quai du Commerce,
1080 Bruxelles;
On the reverse, a colour image from
Google map shows the street view of
23 quai du Commerce
in Brussels in 2017

Shocked by the news of Chantal Akerman's death, American graphic designer Betsy Bickle travelled to Belgium to visit the 23 quai du Commerce in Brussels, the address where Jeanne Dielman, the main character of Akerman's first movie lived. Betsy was denied entry by the current residents. On her return she made this business card and for a year used it to introduce herself to clients, provoking the inevitable confusion and questions that enable her to profess her love of Akerman's œuvre.

A membership card for the
International Flying 15 minutes Club

It is uncertain when the International Flying 15 minutes Club was established by an ever-growing group of transatlantic flight passengers who only watch the first 15 minutes of mainstream movies presented for entertainment onboard of aeroplanes. Their claim is that the 15 minutes contain the entire film, which generally started as a good idea by a single individual to only be corrupted by a team of screenwriters, rewriters, producers, conventions of format, mediocre direction, actors and finally sound conditions and screen size.

According to early member Ayan Salem: 'You know what is going to happen after the first 15 minutes, you really do know that the Hollywood pressure will try to tie all loose ends and explain everything within an hour and a half. It simply is a downhill spiral. Don't be an accomplice to mediocrity, stop the movie when it is still a good idea. Sometimes you have to stop before 15 minutes when it is really bad.'

Membership is free and possession of the card optional.

A Qiblah sticker

You are exhausted from a long flight and after tipping the boy who carried some of your luggage you sink into bed. As usual it is way too soft and would, in the long run, ruin your back but this is a hotel, always short term, softness masquerading as comfort. They make you believe that no one else has clipped their nails, or exchanged fluids in the very same bed you now claim as your own. No edges or colours too strong. The confusion between taste and fear of a statement. Soft colours, soft choices, universally medium. Soft, more flaccid-like. The paintings are painful to watch but this time you feel for the artists, either in a factory somewhere or possibly a real artist who needs the cash and eventually loses the flame for art having discovered its transfiguration into money is the real power. This time you will not get your own paint out and you will not add anything to the painting of this room you'll occupy for the duration of a conference or a workshop in a school. You will not consider hotel rooms as your own exhibition space, seen by hundreds without the audience noticing the work. You will not deface, as subtly and stealthy as a ninja painter, the work of someone else, however soulless it is.

You lie there staring at the ceiling, finding quiet and calm in an ocean of monochrome eggshell punctuated by lights or sometimes a fan, gyrating, trembling, providing a soothing breeze. You are awakened from your zone by an anomaly in the artificial sky. Something is stuck there and you think of a doppelgänger, a like-minded prankster who'd sign their temporary presence by sticking a calling card, Zorro, Arsène Lupin or the more disturbing Zodiac Killer. It has an arrow and you automatically look where it is pointing, the south wall, unadorned by any decoration, without a window, just blank. Nothing. The wall disappears the moment you understand. This sticker the size of a playing card, is, you smile at your own pun, a praying card and the Qiblah. It helps you know where you are in relation to Mecca.

You pray.

The driving license of Karla Lopez

I landed at night in Mexico City. As the buses were still running I decided to take the longer way, resisting the sheltered extension of the taxi drive to my temporary accomodation. People are going home this late — unless, worse, they are going to work this early. It's not as gloomy as the London tube during rush hours, almost jolly in comparison. For all I don't know, they could be going to a party but I doubt it.

At my friend's flat — she is fast asleep — her roommate, who I've not previously met, is chatty, a German expat eager to show me he is local. His notifications are loud and he constantly checks his phone without interrupting his sentences, an evolutionary development to hinder the constant distractions. I only listen, fighting the jet lag. At 3 am he takes off, winking that he's got a Tinder date. Now.

Of the two hours he verbally showered me my brain got excited by one item of information: the possibility of buying a driving license in a certain area of Central Mexico City. This came with a warning: don't go to Tepito. I'm intrigued because I've never been to Mexico but I've heard this from many people as far as Belgium.

The next day I get rid of my work within 24 minutes and am ready to explore. There is a fairly new public bicycle scheme and despite the size of the city I decide to trust whoever thought it would be a good idea to rent bikes to tourists in one of the largest cities in the world.

The difficulty in registering to get access to a public bike gives an idea of how welcome you are as a tourist. In Monaco, you have to subscribe for a minimum of three months and bring a photo, bank statement and ID to a specific address. This is clearly a deterrent.In Stockholm, the difficulty is medium, like a Swedish quality — lagom — and Paris, they want you to actually use it. This was before the bikes you can use geolocalisation to find and unlock with your phone. In Mexico, it is difficult in theory but I am lucky with opening hours and helpful staff.

I deploy the map to check the docking facilities, how well distributed they are and how far it is between them. The centre of Mexico City where the docking bikes are available are in full colour and the areas where you cannot park the bikes are in light grey, immediately showing the status of said neighbourhood among which Tepito is the most famous. Safe Mexico has an inverted capital 'L' shape.

In some places of Parisian suburbs it was not rare to see whole bike docks empty while seeing abandoned bikes around or being used by kids with incredible wheelie skills. I had heard you could unlock them

240

pretty easily and even if they were designed to be rather cumbersome and heavy, they were free. As an ex-shoplifter I understand the twisted ethical logic of stealing from shops and brands rather than the privately owned.

I register for a vehicle and ride straight to the area where, I was told, I could get any official document made within an hour. I have a driving license but know a lot of adults without one. At what age does one give up? None of them took a stance and refused it as a statement. They just never needed one when they were young and find themselves too ashamed to learn but more importantly subject themselves to the humiliating process of having an abusive instructor and later a jury in the back seat empowered with the decision to grant you the freedom of the car.

A perfect present, then, for all my friends whose portrait I can easily find on the internet and Pedro (real name) to make a driving license that apparently works in Mexico but not in the States. They are cheap and makes me wonder how Mexican cops check IDs.

A black and white photocopy the size of a photograph depicting two people as the only visual documentation of five years of one man's life

Do you remember when you took me to this posh restaurant? A surprise for nothing, a surprise even to you, you said then. Two Michelin stars, dressed in everyday clothes. There, all you talked about were two American middle-aged men who meet at a restaurant, having lost touch with one another for years. One listens, one speaks. The listener has a fairly ok career but he does need to write bits and bobs for reviews and other agendas than his own. He works as an actor in a half-hearted but serious way in plays he'd rather write himself. He somehow finds solace in a life that has not fulfilled his ambitious younger self's aspirations he never forgot and silent contemplation has replaced more verbalised provocative monologues with friends.

He is a nice guy and has started looking like one. The other man came back from what seems to be a five-year-long magnificent adventure in experimental theatre which intersected with life to the point that art and work, art and life, art and any other notions one usually use as an obstacle, are becoming one. He has quit the New York scene the listener still belongs to. Is the speaker arguing one can only 'let go and simply embrace this is a ride, the only one and there is no time for a drill?' Is the listener arguing that simple pleasures such as waiting for the bus can equate to being buried alive and becoming one with the Sahara? Is he subconsciously jealous this man pretends having lived what he possibly won't ever know? Is the speaker sharing a positive experience unaware that this seemingly jolly conversation alienates and even further patronises the one who never thought he stayed behind before this conversation?

As we left and you generously paid you showed me a photograph, the only one in five years the speaker possessed. It wasn't a selfie and you can barely recognise him, you said, an emaciated version of himself, sitting next to a young woman with ethnic headgear. They don't even seem to be doing anything, just sitting, emotionless. The bliss must have happened just before of after the snap.

As we walked back home you told me of a formidable experience walking a whole week with 12 students around a lake in Switzerland — so you'd be going forward while making it possible to bring them back to school after a week. You told me they chose not to tell what happened, that they couldn't possibly think of telling a story in a lesser quality than what had been experienced first hand. You told me one participant, once home, immediately grabbed her boyfriend to go back to all the places for the next week, reliving everything with him instead of telling him. On the first night, they stayed at the same fully-automated shower-in-the-corridor rooms as plastic pods cheap motel the group had stumbled across in the middle of the first night a week prior.

At the time, you revealed, the evening had transformed a grim business hotel into a castle of strangers, turned lifelong companions appreciating the warmth of a rough carpet as if it were the throne of gods. The student and her boyfriend, did they feel the same? I asked. Was it even better? I hoped. The group's first night was a Monday, while the couple experienced a Saturday night, when the plastic thin walls of the motorway motel let them noisily know it was used for prostitution. They kept going on for a week but no-one heard about this week either.

A temporary Visa for the Kingdom of
Elgaland-Vargaland, a micro nation born from the
minds of Swedish artists Carl Michael von
Hausswolff and Leif Elggren in 1992

Micro nations are fun. Making up your own country, your own constitution, your own ministries, stamps, uniforms, language, national anthem and dish. Oooh then the flag. Most of them never quite invent anything.

I was in my teens when we played roleplaying games, starting with dungeons and dragons, to cyberpunk, vampire and werewolves, from past, present and future alternative realities. Our dungeon master, the one writing the scenarios we'd interact with, became increasingly creative. I remember him assuming strange voices during a game in which we were elves and knights in search for some treasure. After a whole evening it turned out we were patients in a mental hospital in contemporary Paris believing we were fighting orcs. That got me laughing as movies with twists were all the rage then but my friend Olivier got terribly upset to discover his paladin warrior he developed for three years — twenty in the fiction world — vanished at the whim of the game master.

Heated argument followed, we wanted to be shaken but not tipped overboard the unknown. Later that year this game master became a player and chose to be a creature that was both and neither sex, a plant with a cosmic conscience existing in all realities at once. His behaviour was so disturbing to us that we forced him to choose a more conventional character, revealing how conservative we were. I still wonder if it was coincidental that I quit playing for good a few weeks later.

A piece of paper on which I drew a caterpillar

My neighbour says she remembers feeling happiness when she was 3 years old. I hide the fact that my first memories are from falling through a toilet door and chipping my teeth on the toilet bowl when I was thirteen. Knowing things from the past is one thing, being sure it is a memory another. If you listen to my mother I am the Messiah and she has proof. I don't recall anything that is not from a photograph or a story I have heard. This is why my son only eats basic food while I gorge on exquisites: he won't remember so why bother.

I don't have a son and there is a very vivid memory of waking up in the night and going to the living room, turning the TV on and beginning a movie halfway through. Nothing much happens for a bearable eternity. Women speak an elaborate language I recognise as French but cannot understand. They lie down in the lush grass and observe a caterpillar, which, in turn, seem to observe her for a long interspecies non verbal communicative duration. I fell asleep and have since thought of this movie. I do not seek what it is but in retrospect reckon it's art house quality and I congratulate my eight-year-old self for being part of the intellectual elite.

A wallet printed with the dollar bill design bought in Singapore

I am standing in front of a market stall facing fifty or so currencies on display. Wait, they are fake and I chuckle at the tautological joke: these are wallets for sale with fifty or so currencies printed on them, one for each possible tourist to bring back home. Very clever and for anyone living in a cosmopolitan city like London or Aubervilliers, it's the jackpot of souvenirs. Where I come from, however, it is more common to want to conceal money so the idea of a wallet which looks like a fat wad of cash doesn't quite make sense.

I notice the only wallet franked by a "SPECIMEN" print is the Singaporean wallet, probably nullifying its chance of being purchased.

Whenever travelling abroad I have my local disguise (the extent to which a long-haired Asian person can truly blend with the locals depends on the self-delusion capacity of said tourist). I have a fake Adidas green top (only two stripes) and I pop in any shop to get a plastic bag in which I'll put my wallet and phone, wrapped in a piece of cloth and a small Swiss army knife. The knife is not a weapon but rather a tool-kit to dismantle anything encountered on the street that would possess the potential of transfiguration into a new thing, call it sculpture or toy, what's the difference?

248

I also carry plastic gloves as some of the gold trash is first trash and ziplock free bags from the airport. I was in such disguise in America and had a whole day before a rather important evening meeting already scheduled in a restaurant on Sunset Boulevard. Having finished the necessary computer work in the early hours of the morning, I decided to walk 17 miles to the meeting in what looked like a pleasant day. Perfect temperature. Sunny enough and a whole day of exploration ahead in a city that would surely reject enough for me to scavenge at will.

Seven hours later, I had indeed found many such pieces of valuable trash and had therefore needed to carry more than five plastic bags adorned with the best colourful graphics that mirrored the neighbourhood I walked through: Hispanic, Korean, Italian, Japanese or Armenian. Those bags were in different languages with different visual identities. A mini version of commercial Los Angeles.

The Sun had browned my skin and a thick layer of dust had crystallised from a mixture of sweat, exhaust pipe particles, sand and dead skin. I spotted my friend at the table, looking fresh-faced like a baby who'd just emerged from a five-star air conditioned environment via a limo taxi and stormed directly for a seat, forgetting one would get seated by a waiter. My urgency in visiting the restrooms was such I dumped my bags on the seat opposite him and sign-languaged to him I needed a 'number one'.

On my return he was laughing on his own and told me that once I had disappeared in the toilets a panicked waiter huffily came and said to him, 'Sir I am sorry I will immediately have this homeless man removed from the premises.'

A business-card sized piece of card with the text:
'sculpture pour l'intérieur d'une chaussure,
Max Jenssen 1999'

At the front desk of the MAMCO in Geneva, a transaction occurs: in exchange for 10 Swiss francs one accesses a wonder of contemporary art. Another transaction can happen. A pile of business cards turns out to be a portable caption — 'sculpture for the inside of a shoe'. Next to it is a transparent glass bowl filled with small irregularly-shaped stones. They are not rounded pebbles but rough-edged stones. The invigilator smiles and invites you for a free possession, a true personal encounter with art. Nothing needs additional explanation and you quieten the enthusiastic invigilator by putting your finger on his mouth. You nod at him, he responds. In silence you bend down, take a shoe off and insert a carefully chosen stone, insert your foot next and pocket the caption. Keeping the pain every step of the way, five floors of exhibition while being an artwork yourself, feeling the pain and exhibiting it by adopting a limp walk. On the second floor this woman is limping too. You exchange a knowing glance. When the lights go off, do sculptures stretch and exchange views on visitors?

Mme Vera, resident psychic at the Stanley Hotel, Colorado

Steam engulfs and precedes me into the bedroom. I am wearing the impossibly immaculate white bathrobe and turbanned in the softest towel, which has almost instantly dried my hair. A naked baby is sitting in the middle of the king-size bed. I stop and join the mother, sitting in the corner of the room in the silence required to contemplate what we both recognise as the unique moment rarely if ever seen in any documentary, commented or not by David Attenborough: the becoming of consciousness in the mind of an animal in the transfigurative transition to homo sapiens. IT is touching the remote control and about to figure out IT can empower IT to change the moving image and associated sound on the cumbersome oversized iPad on the wall.

Neither parent is breathing and the miracle happens. We all look at the screen. Whatever appears should not be of any consequence except we recognise the final sequence of Stanley Kubrick's *The Shining* (1980). Both parents jump on the bed to distract the young human from a brilliant, yet possibly disturbing movie for a very tenderage.

We believe there are no coincidences and for a minute, goosebumped at the possibility our child had found *The Shining* since this very hotel was where the book was written by Stephen King. The brochure goes at length to explain this is not the hotel where the movie was shot. It, however, does advertise that room 217 in this hotel is truly haunted and therefore must cost more for any brave guest. Instead of a resident hairdresser or yoga teacher they adequately employ madame Vera, a famous psychic, or so it seems. On the same evening just before dinner an employee of the hotel knocks at the door and proposes a spook tour of the hotel and the haunted off-limit areas. We are bemused but the mother relinquishes her position as only one adult can go while the other stays with the shining baby.

Five or so people are waiting in the lobby at 11pm and a jolly entertainer describes the health and safety regulations of the tour just before introducing with what I can only describe as American enthusiasm that tonight there is a special guest in the person of Kane Hodder, the actor who played the fictional killer Jason Voorhees in the *Friday the 13th* franchise (1980 – ongoing). Although I have seen and enjoyed those I was more familiar with the hockey mask or the disfigured prosthetics of the character than the handsome Burt Reynolds type who suddenly appeared to everyone's explosion of joy at sharing the evening with real ghosts and real fake killer. Moreover they asked us to sign release forms as the actor was accompanied by a crew following him around for his own very special reality TV show.

I do not believe in ghosts, except in Japan. The ambient strength of a whole nation's faith in animism and spirit does create the apparitions and I have personally seen ghosts and felt them in various strongholds of the parallel world, namely deep mountains and near temples, even in urban areas. But this is America and the whole circus was post-modernism at its most absurd. Brilliant, then. I wore my European skepticism and got ready to debunk the mediated supernatural while I should have embraced the ride. It was way past midnight and fatigue made me wonder if it was going to be longer than an hour.

I returned to the room at 7am later terrified and convinced of having seen at least two resident ghosts, having been touched by a cold ethereal creature and paranoid as to whether everyone else was a Daniel Day Lewis level actor pranking me with their own terrors although the fifty bucks I had paid was certainly not enough to create a very convincing reality for a single person. The next day I told everything to the mother who patiently listened and politely refrained from comments. We decided to consult the resident psychic. Her door was shut and we were told she was on vacation.

A 50p coin from 2012

As part of the many events surrounding the 2012 Olympics in London the Bank of England opened a competition for the obverse design of the 50p coin. You might wonder, reading this in the future, what money had to do with international sport and I might congratulate you for both commonsense and naivety but I will also inform you that two of the main sponsors for the the most important gathering of physical athletes across the globe was Coca Cola and McDonalds, two brands your healthier future won't know about. This winning entry and therefore still in circulation simply explains what offside is in football. No further explanation needed.

A 5 euro note with lipstick marks on one side

I once described a wonderful visit to an exhibition to a friend only to realise halfway through that I had never actually seen it for real but read about it close enough to have digested it as my own memory. It was too late to backtrack and shamefully I continued what had transpired to be a lie. And I never looked back. I knew anecdotes I made mine and those feelings, sometimes the physical memory of a smell, the contact of glass or metal from the bad habit of actually touching artworks to commune with them.

Towards the end of my life I had reconstructed enough, forgotten more, inhabited other people's stories, invented the missing links, blamed the infamous suspension of disbelief, conveniently embellished traumatic personal events and created horrors to have hero'd my way through and out, not always as the main character. Nothing that killed me but only what made me stronger. In retrospect I also invented a couple of my own deaths which I obviously survived to tell the stories.

I was poor as a young up and coming actress but luxurious were my ways and highly educated my taste buds. Many times a year I would go to a three-starred restaurant in my best attire, a mink fur coat and the reddest lipstick on my palest of faces. At the end of opulent dinners I would pull out a chequebook, scribble the shameful figure but carefully calligraph my signature to which I would add the love stamp of my lips, as clear as a cartoon, a result of months of exercising at home on napkins stolen from Parisian cafés. Many of those adorn the wall of prestigious establishments in Europe, possibly as a token more valuable than the sum of the unsolved cheques.

An unsigned thank you note from a stranger found in my wallet

I leave little love notes in books whenever I'm in a stranger's home, usually on page 42.

Bloated by the food and drinks of the Christmas celebration I isolate myself and for a whole morning — while everyone is sleeping — I attempt to clean up my mobile phone address book. Who is Christopher or qq5878@gmail.com? There are no last names. The entry for Christopher doesn't even contain any other information. My hangover cannot be blamed for the fact a third of the names ring no bells.

I picked up my friend's book from the table of the bookshop where she would be signing them that afternoon. On the back cover is a flattering, yet accurate picture of her. Against all better judgement my excessive pride motivated my fingers to flick through the pages of actual content to the very end, to the acknowledgements and thanks. Listed by first names in alphabetical order, some individuals I knew well, others not at all. My name was absent.

The rockstar who no longer knows which city he's playing screams, 'Thank you! You know who you are!' I'm in the mosh pit with my best friend. Yes, we do know we are and we shed tears of joy jumping up and down.

I break the fourth paper wall and tell you that I couldn't quite make a list of thank yous. That would be too private for a publication that wishes to reach strangers. For sure, this is composed of other people's works (the artist whose coin is their edition, the designer whose illustration adorns a stamp, the president who refuses to change a face on a banknote, etc.) and also exists because of precedents and serendipity by proximity. Dear R, S, and maybe P, I promise it is neither homage nor rip off, at least intentionally.

I do owe you a thank you for the comment you made, for the suggestion that turned things upside down, for the story you told me (A, F and V, yours are disguised; G and N, yours as you told me). Some thank yous should be tender apologies for writing you out of the story (E, B, P and T). And I do feel that ultimately one should thank parents without whom one wouldn't be and therefore one's actions wouldn't exist but then again where does it end? Let's not forget the dead people who inspired us, or the self-aggrandizing act of gatecrashing a club one wasn't invited to.

Ultimately a thank you list is in this case a dubious exercise at patting oneself on the back of vanity.

I could write a list of people who definitely didn't help instead.

Pick me up card

The obedient Charlotte shops at the local supermarket. Not owning a discount card is her idea of a political act. The purchased items move on the conveyor belt to be held under the scanner for barcode reading. The ritual goes thus. The cashier: 'Do you have a [insert name of the supermarket] card?' 'No,' she replies in a defiance that prevents the cashier to ask the usual second question — 'Would you like one?' Lucky for Charlotte because she couldn't face to say no twice. She obeys because she thinks of herself as positive, that yes is mostly better and she hopes her life will be changed to an endless adventure by the affirmative. She packs her fruits and beers in a tote bag from the Lisson Gallery or the Venice Biennial. She already has the bike lock keys in her hand when she notices a display she could swear wasn't there before. It shows twenty or so different kind of cards, some of discount coupons, others of advertisements, nothing of interest. Except the one that shows a hand and bold letters: PICK ME UP.

The call of destiny is too strong, her hand is already mirroring the image of the hand on the card picking it up. Charlotte said yes, Charlotte has listened to her internal voice reading the simple instructions. The card is already in her pocket and the upper body twists to lead the rest to motion towards the exit but wait, she sees that behind the card is an identical one with the same instructions, equally impossible to resist. 'PICK ME UP', the second card reads, and so she does. This time Charlotte is prepared and she smiles to herself as another card of the same is indeed behind the second she pocketed. She picks her third card and the fourth and the fifth and as if by magic this continues until a perfect dance operates in a silent music, a rhythm an observer could easily compare to the best ballroom dance performance. Nineteen cards later the enjoyable arm dance ceases as instead of another instructional card it is revealed that a piece of plastic with a metal spring was ingenuously pushing the cards forward. Charlotte quickly assimilates the information and leaves the supermarket.

A week or so later, when the fruits and beers were consumed, she comes back to the same supermarket, buys the same items, goes to the same cashier, is disappointed at seeing someone other than the previous employee but is happy to see the card is back. Her arms know the drill, she positions herself at the perfect distance to execute what is asked of her — to PICK ME UP. This time only seven cards.

During the week her thoughts are consumed by the excitement to return and pick up more cards but she cannot break the rules so awaits for the real need for consumption.

On her third visit she hits gold: 36 cards; on her seventh, only one but over six months she accumulates 378 of the cards. It is now June and Charlotte almost runs to her supermarket, the happiness of repetition, the call of the cards, the calling card, she pays for her food and looks at the display, letting go of a small laughter by herself for herself some strangers around ignore even if when they meet their friends later they will mention the nutter they saw in a shop.

Shock and horror there are no cards this time and Charlotte stands for a full minute, a long time in such a place, before going home.

The cards never came back.

Found at the reception of a hotel in the Netherlands in the late teens of the twenty-first century. You, reader, from my future, listening inside of your head to this, from the back of a fully-automated vehicle, can you imagine my excitement at testing what I only had seen in sci-fi movies? I'd be in the back of an empty Tesla, speaking to the car itself, an artificial intelligence I could converse with while my body would be moved from point A to point B.

My rule is to never get in a taxi if there is public transport but this was a glimpse into the future, stepping into me older while being the same age, remembering me younger watching teleportation or flying cars enacted on screen. I called, expecting a disembodied voice chosen by the AI having identified who I am and adapting language, vocabulary, tone and mood based on my latest presence on the internet, making me feel at home, relaxed in the knowledge a friend was taking this call and would even drive me to a destination they would deduct from my internet footprint. The operator would… finish my sentences and this techno experience would only cost the fare of a cab ride.

A rude woman answered the call to tell me that no taxis were available before an hour and that no, they had human drivers.

The father is standing in an underground corridor smelling of a constantly updated communal fart of commuting bodies using the metro to go back and forth to jobs most found meaning in — money and therefore their bi-annual holy days of respite.

Next to the father is the daughter, her face at an even worse level of the commuters' bums, origins of the odourants remnants of human made wind giving unsolicited olfactory information of the insides of strangers. The daughter is still young enough to analyse smells from an objective perspective and hasn't decided whether it does indeed stink.

The daughter is wondering why the all-powerful adult next to her — the best person and her personal favourite among humankind except the mother who is at the very exact same height — shows signs of anxiety she barely recognises. The father has worked all his life to free himself from the constraints of obligation. By this he means having the choice to say no.

No, he won't obey to a god. No, he doesn't need a job he dislikes. No he can walk away from boring conversations. No he won't go to war for a government he won't vote for and certainly won't vote against as it is fashion. No he won't queue. No he won't be obliged to be physically constrained in prison.

Therefore abiding the law, the sad reality of freedom, somehow. The father is old but he feels young. He looks at his daughter and smiles a disfigured rictus as if to claim everything's a mistake and they will soon resume their journey.

The people in green uniforms have stopped the father and the daughter. They have asked them to stay against the wall while arresting other humans who join the position. Some protest, some try to go through the barrage of bodies but the uniformed humans are prepared and similar to a rugby team possess different body shapes for the situation. The big muscly ones, a head taller than the ones with electronic fine printing machines, are a wall. The people standing know why they must obey as the anti-social behaviour of travelling without a ticket in the French metro costs millions to the honest population.

The father thinks fast. He has a valid ticket. In his wallet are three reduced price tickets for children and seven for adults. Only his own has been franked by the electronic gates because the reduced tickets were demagnetised. Add to this that in the UK children go for free, he could use a thick English accent to prove he doesn't quite know the customs of this beautiful city of Lumières he brought his daughter to visit for the first time. He knows, however, that his daughter will contradict him and she'd be right to find his accent amusing and would tell the controller in minute details of the countless times she has visited Paris. Nevertheless, if intentions are different from facts the uniformed humans are humans and would perhaps warm to the story that indeed he possess three tickets that didn't work, that the entrance he went through wasn't (wo)manned because of automatisation and oh my, where is this robot replacing of humans going?

Luckily you and I still have jobs artificial intelligence won't be able to do or come to think of it they probably will. Yes he could have bought another ticket from the machine or even used an adult ticket but officer, as anyone else here, we just tried to get to point B using the fantastic transport system, an engineering miracle of efficiency which, let's admit, is here to serve the humans to stay the least time within its corridors, platforms and trains and allow to visit museums or quickly go home to the arms of their beloved families.

The father is going to argue with friendly bulletpoints. He is old enough to know this should be said in a calm and friendly voice with a smile. He identifies the boss. She is young, of African origin, probably third or fourth generation and unlike most people who do this job, good looking. The father backtracks the last thoughts and is happy nobody heard him think. He fights his terrible preconceptions that young people are more tolerant, less conservative, more human, able to listen to stories. His heart sinks at how stupid he is, thinking of the shared non-whiteness between her — for once empowered and the boss of an otherwise very male and white team — and him, someone mostly called Jackie Chan on any street. Surely she knows at first glance that the father, despite being born in France, like her, was at school the Chinese of his class, only hanging out with the Arabs and the Portuguese.

Although Alexis, while being Portuguese was, already at 6 years of age the most handsome of the school, allowing inherent racist thoughts by all other kids to recess and allow him the god-like status he probably still enjoys (Alexis, what have you become?). And to add shame to injury he even flirts with the idea of using his daughter's cuteness to get out of this forced custody situation. The daughter has been looking at her father all the while and has guessed it all. She hugs him as if to say, well, we are guilty or rather you are so do bite the bullet and be the father I need.

A silver drachma with the owl of Athena chiselled
out of a greek euro coin

Weddings are conservative and it's best to keep
your mouth shut about this opinion. Don't mention
you don't believe in getting married, especially avoid
adding: 'Well, it's my opinion anyway, you guys are
good, you should do it.' Don't complain it will be at
the church, that the food should have been simpler,
after all you're happy it conventionally features well-
dressed people who will unsurprisingly get trashed
on wine and end up naked in the swimming pool.

And there was the stretched limo and before you
could question why women couldn't come to the
stag night, there you are, the five friends who try
to befriend the sober driver, a really nice guy, that
Simon, definitely could be one of us in the back,
playing the cliché. It is our cliché so give us a break.
Stretch limo once and never again so let's enjoy it at
least. The night is eventful with non-events. Nobody
can remember a thing nor would want to as it is just a
succession of unchallenging automatisms that proves
the Matrix is real. We have no will nor soul and worst
of all we loved it.

The next day is erased and fast forwarded to day
three when Sam (okay, that's me) has the idea of piling
rocks on the stretch limo while Hassan paints the car
with thick acrylic, choosing the same colour as what

268

he is painting. Despite Jean-Claude's continuous and repetitive plea that French artist Bertrand Lavier did that ages ago no one cares and anyway a prank is not art when it's not in a white cube. It logically ends by a brick in the window and amazingly we hotwire the car to start based on the whimsical knowledge we have from movies. For some reason we don't categorise this as stealing and we drive to the next town where we carefully park the limo on the church carpark. We have found the driver's mobile phone and it rings. We pick up but don't speak. Hassan suddenly remembers the car actually belongs to the driver, not a company, guilt clouds enter us.

Did you ever feel you were already too far on the other side? That the situation cannot be reversed and everything is new from then on, that perhaps it should just be pushed and let's enter the oneway tunnel. I remember watching Juliette Lewis and Woody Harrelson in *Natural Born Killers*, I remember watching Martin Sheen and Sissy Spacek in *Badlands* and I remember reading about Florence Rey and Audry Maupin, the young cop killers of Paris, all in the confusion of fiction and reality, what influences which. In our case it wasn't a sense of injustice or anger but of an absurd logic we constructed between us.
The driver had come to the Church and we hid, laughing delusional at the brilliance of our prank, never

in doubt this was fun, despite the sweaty face of Simon and his eyes that revealed this was tragedy. Have you ever noticed comedy movies are just real life tragedies?

Hassan, Benoît and Jean-Claude left. I stayed two more days with Martin in the desert, picking up debris and throwing them at each other. What a game. Two local kids, possibly 15 or 16, passed us and asked for money in such a forceful manner we refused. They stared at us quietly for a terrifying minute and eventually disappeared.

Martin and I were walking on a straight road, both sides fenced by barbed wires although we could only see the endless desert on the other sides. In this strange corridor without a roof we saw two camels approaching us. It was the two kids. We were going towards them, them towards us, the confrontation would be inevitable and we had not seen anyone for a few hours. The car was two miles from where we were and worst of all I could see Martin was scared — oh no, Martin, I just wanted to see you were in control. Stupidly I picked up a hubcap while trying to avoid eye contact with the camel riders. My whole body suddenly exuded sweat when I saw they both were armed with their shirts in which they tied a stone.

I only remember closing my eyes, shielding myself with a broken hubcap bearing the violent hits, anticipating the sting of suffering the blows. Not the head, not the head.

In my fist, clenched, was a drachma coin I had chiselled out of a Greek euro coin.

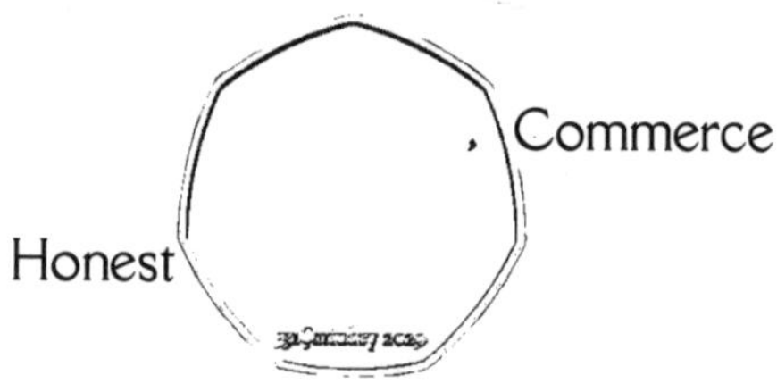

Does this text contain inaccurate information or language that you feel we should improve or change?